Praise for The Awakened Leader: One Simple Leadership Style That Works Every Time, Everywhere

---

***"Awakened Leader** is wonderful. It just may 'awake' us all from our slumbers and the nightmare organizations from which we are all suffering."*

—Ian Mitroff
Author, *A Spiritual Audit of Corporate America: A Hard Look at Spirituality, Religion, and Values in the Workplace*
J-B Warren Bennis Series

"I really encourage you to deeply pause as you read this book. Quickly reading this book and depositing lots of ideas into your head will give you some awakening with a small "a." However, taking your time, deeply pausing, and reflecting as things come up can potentially elicit some authentic awakening with a capital "A." This book can be a transformational awakening—it is up to you."

—Kevin Cashman
Founder and CEO, LeaderSource, Inc.
Author, *Leadership from the Inside Out* and *Awakening the Leader Within*

In a world of distraction and 'busy-ness' it is hard to stay awakened. Yet, many leaders want to become just that.* The Awakened Leader *shows readers how they can use ancient wisdom in a new world. Wake up and read this book!

—Marshall Goldsmith
Founder and CEO, Marshall Goldsmith Partners LLC
Author, *The Leader of the Future* and *What Got You Here Won't Get You There*

It's high time for leaders everywhere to awake, arise, and adopt a classic style that works anywhere.

—Ken Shelton
Editor, Leadership Excellence
Author, *Beyond Counterfeit Leadership*, *Real Success*, and *One-on-One: Conversations with Stephen Covey*

In* The Awakened Leader, *Dr. Marques advises leaders on how to pay better attention to their whole experience so that they can improve themselves, their organizations, and the world.

—Martin Wilcox
Director of Publications
Center for Creative Leadership

Joan Marques

The Awakened Leader: One Simple Leadership Style That Works Every Time, Everywhere

The Awakened Leader: One Simple Leadership Style That Works Every Time, Everywhere

Published by

BOOKS FOR ALL THAT YOU ARE
PERSONHOOD PRESS

P.O. Box 370
Fawnskin, CA 92333
800-429-1192
personhoodpress@att.net
www.personhoodpress.com

ISBN: 1-932181-24-5

Cover Design: Linda Jean Thille – Blackstone Arts
Printed in the United States of America

This book is dedicated to all those leaders who showed me through their actions and words what Awakened Leadership should and should not be about.

May this work be a source of inspiration to all of you.

Contents

Foreword

While it may sound a bit dramatic, leadership is an immortal yet ever relevant topic. Has there ever been a time when awakened leadership was not crucial to a civilization's existence? Has there ever been a more crucial time than the present for more awakened leaders?

Leadership is *not* a job, a task, a role, or a level on an organizational chart. *Leadership is a sacred calling to make a life-enriching difference in the world.* A beautiful and inspiring story from the Talmud illustrates the point: "Every blade of grass in all of creation has an angel bent over it whispering three words of encouragement—Grow. . .Grow. . . Grow." Whatever our belief system, most of us can relate to the impulse to grow. The impulse to grow as people. . .to grow as a family. . .to grow as a team. . .to grow as a society—this impulse to grow is the evolutionary pull of life itself. When we are awake to this impulse to be more, to grow more, to contribute more, then we open ourselves to the possibility of making a greater contribution to all those we touch.

As leaders and people, we are all "awake" to a certain degree. The question is, "What are we awake to?" Are we primarily awake to our ego, our self-interest, our fears, our image, our success? If ego, self-interest, and fear are the masters of our identity, then our leadership will play out in a certain way. Arrogance, control, domination, and a scarcity mentality will likely be the resultant behaviors. On the other hand, if we are more awake to our deepest essence as a person, focused on serving the needs of others, and if we have faith/trust that is bigger than just about any circumstance we face, then a whole new set of behaviors come forth from our more deeply awakened leadership. So the real question of awakening is this: *Are we awake to our light that serves or to our shadow that copes*?

We recently worked with a team at a global firm that thought they "had it all together." On one level they did, as the fastest growing company in a high-growth industry—everything on the surface looked great. They were very "awake" to getting results. However, the underlying dynamics were not so pretty. Lack of trust, entrenched silos, dysfunctional competition were all the by-products of not being "awake" to the factors that could sustain their success. As a result of some intensive individual and team coaching, the team was able to see how its winning formula of "results at all costs" needed to be expanded to "results + people = sustainable performance." Individually and collectively, they woke up. Is this type of awakening just a "nice thing," or can research demonstrate that it produces a tangible, measurable business benefit?

Fortunately, over the past several years much research has appeared to support the value of awakened, developed leaders and teams. Goleman, Zenger & Folkman, Collins, and many others have contributed greatly to the evidence. As described in the book *Extraordinary Leader,* Zenger & Folkman analyzed 6,000 leaders whose main competency was results, versus leaders whose main strength was people. What do you think they found? Actually, there was *no* statistical difference between these two groups. The results-oriented leaders got to the 90th percentile of leadership effectiveness in their organization 13 percent of the time, while the people-oriented leaders did it 9 percent of the time. So what about the leader who had results and people competencies? These leaders got to the 90th percentile of leadership effectiveness in their organizations 66 percent of the time—a quantum leap in performance! Research increasingly supports the fact that good leaders are awake to results, but great leaders are awake to people and results.

So how do we become more awake as leaders? As far as I can tell from coaching thousands of leaders and teams globally, there appears to be no end to becoming more awake, more developed as a person and as a leader. So if there is no end to awakening, how do we go from our current state of development to the next state? We awaken through the Power of Pause. The Pause Principle℠ is the counter-intuitive dynamic of becoming more by doing less. To achieve a breakthrough (whether it is personal, psychological, spiritual, interpersonal, scientific, strategic, or commercial) requires a process of stepping back in order to more powerfully go forward. The archer pulls the bow back to create a more powerful shot. The leader conducts an off-site to create a new strategy. The scientist takes a shower and suddenly the insight comes. A high potential manager reviews a 360° and commits to stepping forward in a new way. We meditate and get ready to face life in a new, more resilient manner. To get to another level, we pause, step back, reframe, and face life anew. Pause creates awakening: Pause gives resilience, new perspectives, new creativity, and new breakthrough. We *pause through* in order to *break through*. We pause to awaken to new possibilities.

I really encourage you to deeply pause as you read this book. Quickly reading this book and depositing lots of ideas into your head will give you some awakening with a small "a." However, taking your time, deeply pausing, and reflecting as things come up can potentially elicit some authentic awakening with a capital "A." This book can be a transformational awakening—it is up to you.

In addition to encouraging you to pause deeply as you read this book, I would also encourage you to practice deeply once you finish the book. Awakening without practice is a fool's journey. The Tao Te Ching puts it this way, "The fool merely admires the Tao while the wise practices the Tao." Find two to three key things you will commit to practice and stick with them for three to four months. Establish your awakening practices, then move onto a couple more. Practice makes awakening a living, breathing, day-to-day reality.

Treat this book as a genuine developmental journey—an inspiring yet pragmatic way to further your "sacred calling to make a difference in the world."

Kevin Cashman
Founder & CEO, LeaderSource, Inc.
Author of *Leadership from the Inside Out*
and *Awakening the Leader Within*

Author's Prologue

Indira Gandhi, former prime minister of India, once said,

> *"My grandfather once told me that there were two kinds of people: those who do the work and those who take the credit. He told me to try to be in the first group. There is much less competition."*

As you read about the Awakened Leader and the qualities this person harbors, I'd like you to think of the above statement. Awakened Leaders know that when you work hard, you earn respect from those who work with you. You become more aware of what's going on in your surroundings, and you find more fulfillment.

There's so much captured in hard work, particularly if done diligently and with purpose. When you as a leader demonstrate that you're not above assisting your followers when and where needed, you make a powerful statement—and you claim their esteem, support, and belief in you. There are many talkers in the world who know everything about giving orders, but little about ensuring success through personal input. Awakened Leaders differ from them.

The "Awakened Leader"

The first thing we have to do is to return to life, to wake up and be mindful of each thing we do.
Thich Nhat Hanh

It's important to realize that wakefulness is key to survival today. Confinements don't work anymore. We all operate globally, deliberately or not. Increasingly, we all confront diversity: people from different backgrounds, age groups, mindsets, and traditions. Gone are the days when we could study specific categories of followers and then be set for the rest of our careers. If we're not flexible today, we'll be pushed aside tomorrow.

Awakened Leadership requires us to stop sleeping and refrain from dwelling obsessively on past or future. Unfortunately, there are still very few among us who practice the art of being awake. Everybody seems so busy keeping up with everybody else that they forget to access their greatest internal qualities. They forget to turn inward *first* so that they can find out what *their* purpose is in life. They go with the flow without taking the time to think whether they even *like* the flow. As Ralph Waldo Emerson once remarked, "Many people would rather die than think."

Awakened Leaders are among those who *do* take the time to think. They're among those who *do* invest effort to reconnect with their core, and then connect with others.

If you don't want to become obsolete, this book is for you—not just for now, but for the rest of your life.

Chapter 1:

What is an Awakened Leader?

The simplest explanation of an
Awakened Leader is:
"A leader who is awake."

Not just in the factual sense of the
word, but in every way.

As an Awakened Leader you
maintain a high level of alertness
in every regard:

Toward yourself and your driving
motives in various matters;

Toward the people you guide;
toward the organization you lead;

Toward the environment in which
your organization operates, and

Toward the entire universe.

What's Ahead

This chapter presents some inspirational impulses toward Awakened Leadership, generated through conversation and readings. To clarify the concept of Awakened Leadership, we'll then take a walk through history and into the present, reviewing examples of Awakened Leadership. This chapter also reviews elements of Awakened Leadership, emphasizing authenticity and emotional intelligence, as they're so crucial to this leadership style. Finally, the chapter reviews the three dimensions of Awakened Leadership—internal, external, and integrated—presenting models for further clarification.

Inspiration from a Meeting

During a lunch meeting a few years ago, a dear friend, Richard, shared with me five life rules that I thought could form the basis of a book about Awakened Leadership:

1. Goals are important, but the journey should be the main source of joy. It's all about the journey. Reaching your goal is just a small part of the victory; you have to make everyday of the trip worthwhile, since you spend most of your time "traveling" anyway.

2. Follow the suggestion of Joe Simonetta from his book *Seven Words That Can Change the World:* Be healthy, be kind, respect the environment. Richard explained to me that being healthy refers to your responsibility toward yourself; being kind, to your relationship with other living beings; and respecting the environment, to your interconnectedness with everything and everyone around you.

3. Don't underestimate your intuition. Recognize it, and listen to it—not in a wild and disjointed way, but in sync with the rationality of everything you've learned. But don't try to quantify everything, for quality is what it's all about. If

you learn to respect your intuition, you'll find yourself happier and much more content.

4. Everything comes at the right time. It's a wave, a flow. No need to push or force. The way you conduct yourself and treat others will determine the way they see you. In this regard, Richard gave a few examples of friendly contacts he'd made in the previous months and how advantageous they'd turned out. Yes, life certainly has a way of showing you that the "what goes around comes around" rule is still very much in effect!

5. Make sure that everything you do is in line with your deepest conviction. If you take a step back and analyze what it is you're doing, it should all boil down to the one principle you strongly belief in. If that's not the case, you should consider where, how, and why you went astray.

The beauty of spending time with people like Richard is, beside the points they make through their words, their actions teach you some additional lessons. This is what my friend's behavior taught me that day:

- Help people to feel good about themselves, because it will set them at ease and ultimately bring out the best in them. Richard's positive remarks regarding my appearance and my perceived strength encouraged me to open up and talk freely about all areas of my life. I found myself easily unfolding my plans for the future, supported by his enthusiasm and the obvious synergy between us.

- Know your friends well enough to meet them in an environment where they'll feel most comfortable. In order to do this, you have to obtain insight into the interests of the other party, which has a lot to do with empathy and emotional intelligence.

- You're as young as you feel, and you're certainly never too old to start something new. The very act of taking on new challenges will keep you healthy and prevent physical, spiritual, mental, and psychological decline.

- Building integrity is invaluable in establishing and maintaining rewarding relationships.

- Be patient. Some initiatives, plans, or strategies will move like a rocket, and others will need time to take off. Just don't try to push the slow starters harder than they can handle because that could lead to untimely destruction of something that might have been good if only you had given it enough opportunity to evolve.

- Do what you have to do, even if it's not the most desired activity you can think of at the moment. Always know your focus—it will help you to realize your goals, step by step, day by day. As long as you know where you're going, you won't get lost in mediocrity.

Although the memorable meeting with my friend lasted only 90 minutes, the lessons will last a lifetime. Like all Richard's lessons, these stuck in my mind and my heart. They're very much in line with the behavior of an Awakened Leader. The following pages will demonstrate that behavior in more detail.

Inspiration from Readings

As leadership theory continues to develop, there's one theme that encompasses all: cognizance, or the very act of being awake. When you review some popular leadership styles such as team leadership, strategic leadership, symbolic leadership, and servant leadership, you find that the foundation to successful implementation of all these styles is **applicability**. In other words: each of these leadership styles will only succeed at the right time, in the right situation, and with the right people.

This observation is nothing new. Many authors have claimed before that there's no single leadership style that proves to be successful under all circumstances. For instance, in their book *Leadership: Enhancing the Lessons of Experience*, Hughes, Ginnett, and Curphy maintain that leadership depends on several factors such as the situation and the followers, and the leader's qualities or characteristics. These authors also warn that we shouldn't automatically jump to conclusions about a leader strictly on the basis of the behavior he or she demonstrates—it could be the right way to behave "in *that* context with *those* followers."

Among the many other authors who've arrived at a similar conclusion is Warren Bennis, who explains in his 2003 article, "Flight of the Phoenix," that genuine leaders empathize with others, engage them in shared meaning, and make them feel essential. Bennis states further that no single style has a lock on the ability to win others to a vision.

There are numerous other sources that underscore this point, but we'll look at two more. In an interview published in *New Zealand Management*, Professor William Rosenbach of Gettysburg College states, "What leaders do is important, but how they do it is of equal concern. Although much research has focused on identifying the one best style, no single style or personality is best for all situations."

Finally, in a *Journal of Management Inquiry* article, "Where Have All The Leaders Gone?" Madsen and Hammond put it this way: "The monolithic, one-size-fits-all theory of leadership that's a result of globalization and the primacy of the American management model must be broken. It doesn't work anywhere; it doesn't work in the US."

The above citations illustrate general agreement on the fact that the situation and the type of followers involved play a significant role in the leadership style that will be successful.

Now, considering the multifaceted nature of Awakened Leadership precisely based on the requirements mentioned above—the situation and the followers—especially in the context of all stakeholders and the environment at large, we could see Awakened Leadership as one leadership style that is directly applicable in all scenarios.

Two of the authors cited above, Madsen and Hammond, slightly touched on this perspective when they described an emerging self-organizing process in taking localized actions to achieve global impact. It is exactly this *self-organizing* process, this *all-inclusive* and *well-considered specific strategy tailored to local circumstances*, that forms the foundation of Awakened Leadership.

Historical Indications of Awakened Leadership

Awakened Leadership is not a new practice. Buddha, still revered as a role model and leader after 2,500 years, is an excellent example. In *Teachings of the Buddha*, Jack Kornfield describes a remarkable encounter between Buddha and another man that occurred just after Buddha's enlightenment. The man was struck by Buddha's extraordinary radiance and peaceful presence, and asked whether Buddha was a celestial being, a god, a magician, or a wizard. When Buddha denied each description, the man asked, "Well, are you a man?" Even to this Buddha said, "No." The man finally called out, "Well, my friend, then what are you?" Buddha replied, "I am awake."

The fact that Buddha's teachings still have traction today shows us how timeless they are. And although it may be a bit far-fetched to think of ourselves as enlightened, we can still exhibit enlightened behavior if we want to work on it. That's what Awakened Leadership is about.

In fact, although not specifically designating it as such, many leaders have practiced the timeless principles of Awakened Leadership. Jesus Christ, for instance, seemed to have a great connection with his disciples, yet at the same time was available to the needy and downtrodden in the places he visited. Through his multifaceted, highly alert, and empathetic approach, Jesus Christ demonstrated Awakened Leadership.

Mother Teresa, who set up an order called the Missionaries of Charity, is another great example of an Awakened Leader in her own right. The order Teresa created specialized in alleviating the needs of rejected ones everywhere. There was Gandhi, who sacrificed his law practice to devote his life to the improvement of living conditions in India. And there was Dr. Martin Luther King, who engaged in the dangerous task of guiding the civil rights movement in the United States.

You could, of course, raise questions about these leaders' private lifestyles, but there's no doubt that they had some crucial elements in common such as empathy, the ability to see the bigger picture, perseverance and determination, flexibility, humility, but also hard work and a strong sense of fairness. In that sense, they practiced Awakened Leadership, guiding followers from hopelessness to betterment.

Awakened Leadership in Modern Times

"I suppose leadership at one time meant muscles; but today it means getting along with people."
Mohandas Gandhi

In a time where everyone—individuals, business corporations, and nonprofit organizations—operates globally, whether they want to or not, it profits them to consider the significance and advantages of Awakened Leadership.

With the rapidly spreading tendencies of outsourcing and the global search for the most profitable resources, production locations, and markets, and with the continuous advancement of the Internet, every leadership style that focuses on a single type of situation or followers has become obsolete.

The flexibility requirement of leadership is nothing new either. As Smircich and Morgan wrote 24 years ago, "Leaders are those individuals who are capable of taking an ambiguous situation and framing it in a meaningful and acceptable way for the followers." That's the practice of Awakened Leadership in a nutshell. The massive confrontations we face today with members of different cultures, along with dealing inevitably with different viewpoints, customs, and procedures as a result, don't leave us much choice but to adapt if we want to be successful in the near and far future.

Practicing Awakened Leadership starts with a change in your motives and perspectives, along with the realization that everything on Earth is interconnected. A simple leaf from a tree is a good example: how could it become a leaf without the tree, air, water, and the right temperature? The leaf could exist through the process of what Thich Nhat Hanh, a Vietnamese monk, calls *interbeing*. Think of yourself. You're a good example of interbeing as well. In order to survive, you need water, air, sun, affection, and the products that others make. You depend on and are part of your environment. And your environment depends on and is part of you.

Your first step toward wakefulness should be the understanding that everything *you* do ultimately affects *everyone* else in the world; every harm you ignore, you ultimately approve of; and you, like everybody else, have the responsibility to make your surroundings, and ultimately your world, a better place in the interest of all who live there, as well as in your "enlightened" self-interest.

This also entails that, if you commit some kind of injustice, no matter if no one sees or knows it, you're ultimately harming the world, and therefore yourself. If you allow injustice to happen by simply shrugging it off as none of your business, you actually assent to it.

The whole difference lies in your attitude. What do you do, and what do you refrain from doing? What do you use as your driving motives? If you're planning on starting a new business, for instance, will you first think of how much money you can make, regardless of the effect your business will have on society—like most businesses did 40 or 50 years ago? Or will you *first* look at the benefit you can create for your surroundings, and *then* how you can make it economically profitable? If you want to practice Awakened Leadership, you'll always contemplate the effects of your actions on the quality of life around you before you act. Additionally, if you want to be an Awakened Leader you'll never engage in a venture that causes harm to any part of your environment, regardless of how distant that part may seem from your sand box.

The world's richest man, Bill Gates, in his post-Microsoft days, is a good example of the fact that it's never too late to start practicing Awakened Leadership. After years of cut-throat competition in the information technology industry and engagement in practices that some still may not have forgiven him, Gates has chosen a different path. He has assigned himself the global task of utilizing his intelligence and insights in order to serve peoples and organizations that need them. And he's so good at it that other billionaires such as Warren Buffett are starting to trust him with the administration of their philanthropy as well.

Engaging in Awakened Leadership entails developing the proper knowledge, intelligence, or connections to accomplish any task. Skills, education, knowledge, and experience are of tremendous importance in our world today. You won't get far without some knowledge that distinguishes you from the large crowd and provides you the confidence, conviction, and reputation of being an authority in your field. You don't have to look to big names such as Bill Gates, Donald Trump, or Oprah Winfrey, although they're splendid examples of the power of skills, education, knowledge, and experience in their fields—you can find examples right in your workplace or home too. Those around you who ever achieved anything first obtained the appropriate skills, education, knowledge, and experience needed to achieve their goals.

However, before anything else you want to make sure that you utilize your skills toward issues that will advance the *quality of life in general*, because, ultimately, this will benefit you as well.

The good news is that an increasing number of today's leaders are gaining consciousness about the fact that profits become much more rewarding when they're obtained as a *logical result* of conscious endeavors rather than as a *driving motive*.

This consciousness is in line with the practices of Awakened Leaders: They're capable of seeing the macro and the micro picture at the same time. They consider the impact of their actions over the short, medium, and long term. And they do that for every living being involved, even those that don't reside within their immediate circle.

The following sections provide a step-by-step analysis of what Awakened Leadership is about.

Elements of Awakened Leadership

"Do not wait for leaders.
Do it alone, person-to-person."
Mother Teresa

The first question that might come up when we think about Awakened Leadership is: What exactly does it entail? The simplest answer would be: Awakened Leadership entails every leadership style, trait, and skill that's applicable and advantageous to all parties involved.

Let's review some styles involved in Awakened Leadership. Awakened Leadership entails, among others, the three basic leadership styles listed by Curtin in his 1995 article "The 'gold collar' leader...?":

1) Autocratic, in which the leader issues detailed orders and expects them to be carried out automatically;
2) Laissez-Faire, in which the leader tolerates subordinates to virtually do as they please;

3) Democratic, in which the leader allows workers to participate in decision-making.

Yet, there's more to Awakened Leadership than the above. Servant leadership, for instance, is also an important factor of Awakened Leadership as long as the environment is receptive to it. Wikipedia, the online encyclopedia, describes servant leadership as a style that emphasizes the leader's role as steward of the resources (human, financial, and otherwise) provided by the organization. It encourages leaders to serve others while staying focused on achieving results in line with the organization's values and integrity.

Being aware of all available options, an Awakened Leader will first evaluate the followers and the circumstances, and then implement the style that's most appropriate.

Leadership practitioners may now contest that all of this greatly resembles situational leadership. Indeed, Awakened Leadership comprises all of the elements of situational leadership as Northouse describes them in his book *Leadership Theory and Practice*: "The essence of situational leadership demands that a leader matches his or her style to the competence and commitment of subordinates."

However, Awakened Leadership does not end with the situational approach. It goes beyond situational. To get a sense of how far beyond, first we need to look at some traits of Awakened Leaders.

In his 2001 article, "The Conscious Leader," Secretan touches on the most important aspect of Awakened Leadership: consciousness—or as we refer to it here, wakefulness. Secretan defines consciousness as being awake to the mystical and ineffable aspects of being alive. He then highlights the difference between a rational and a conscious mind in stating that the rational mind sees a world of scarcity and responds with fear, whereas the conscious mind sees a world of abundance and responds with love.

In an earlier article titled, "A unified theory of leadership: Experiences of higher states of consciousness in world-class leaders," Harung, Heaton, and Alexander also address the importance of wakefulness in leaders, stating that a more abstract and universal feature of leaders is their heightened degree of consciousness or wakefulness.

Aside from the foundational element of wakefulness or consciousness, Kirkpatrick and Locke's six leadership traits form an important set of characteristics of the practice of Awakened Leadership: 1) the desire to lead, 2) honesty, 3) integrity, 4) self-confidence, 5) cognitive ability, and 6) knowledge of the business.

As in everything, balance is crucial in the application of Awakened Leadership. Along with selecting the appropriate style and developing distinctive traits, Awakened Leaders should maintain a responsible balance between the two main types of leadership behavior: task and relationship. Northouse clarifies these types as follows: Task-motivated leaders are concerned primarily with reaching a goal, whereas relationship-motivated leaders are concerned with developing close interpersonal relations.

Although most people will tend to say that relationship orientation is the best way to go, we need to realize that there are situations where a task approach is the best way to get things done. Especially in crisis situations, or when time is of the essence, a goal-oriented focus can make a significant difference.

Groundwork for presenting a complete model of Awakened Leadership requires discussion of two additional characteristics: emotional intelligence and authenticity—characteristics extremely important to our increasingly complicated work and living environment.

Emotional Intelligence

There's no Awakened Leadership without emotional intelligence. While there still doesn't seem to be one solid, concise definition of emotional intelligence because the term is relatively new, Wikipedia offers a pretty decent formulation of what it entails, describing emotional intelligence as "*an ability, capacity, or skill to perceive, assess, and manage the emotions of one's self, of others, and of groups.*"

Daniel Goleman has written intensely about emotional intelligence. In his article "The emotionally competent leader," Goleman defines emotional intelligence as "*the ability to rein in emotional impulses, to read another's innermost feelings, and to handle relationships and conflict smoothly.*[DGH1]" Emphasizing the importance of developing and sustaining this quality, Goleman explains that these emotional aptitudes can preserve relationships, protect one's health, and improve success at work.

Goleman divides emotional intelligence into five competencies:

1) The ability to identify and name one's emotional states and to understand the link between emotions, thought, and action;

2) The capacity to manage one's emotional states—to control emotions or to shift undesirable emotional states to more adequate ones;
3) The ability to enter into emotional states (at will) associated with a drive to achieve and be successful;
4) The capacity to read, be sensitive to, and influence other people's emotions;
5) The ability to enter and sustain satisfactory interpersonal relationships.

In another article, Mayer, Caruso, and Salovey explain emotional intelligence as an ability to recognize the meanings of emotion and their relationships, and to reason and problem-solve on that basis. These authors conclude that emotional intelligence is involved in the capacity to perceive emotions, assimilate emotion-related feelings, understand the information of those emotions, and manage them.

The above explanations underscore the significance of emotional intelligence as a crucial element in the performance of Awakened Leadership.

Authenticity

The final attribute we'll consider before presenting the model for Awakened Leadership is authenticity. Bill George, retired CEO from Medtronic, describes this style of leading as "*driven by passion and purpose, not greed.*[DGH2]" George keys on five essential dimensions to authentic leaders: purpose, values, heart, relationships, and self-discipline. He perceives authentic leadership as the only way to build lasting value by focusing on the company's missions, customers, and employees. George also explains the creation and sustenance of lasting value by referring to various aspects that we'll divide here into two distinctive categories: 1) the people, and 2) the organization.

Pertaining to the people aspect, George stresses important behaviors such as

- connecting every day with your employees;
- being out with your customers to look for great ideas for growth;
- getting results for all your stakeholders, not just the shareholder of the past five minutes.

Pertaining to the well-being of the organization, George lists the following behaviors:

- building your business by pursuing your mission with a passion;

- being true to your core values in every decision;
- building an enduring organization of authentic leaders from top to bottom.

This is as far as we'll go for now on the topic of authenticity, although we'll return to the topic because, just as with emotional intelligence, there is no Awakened Leadership without authenticity.

Based on the above review of the styles and behaviors critical to Awakened Leadership, we can now posit a comprehensive definition of Awakened Leadership:

Awakened Leadership is the all-encompassing leadership approach involving the leader's awareness to incorporate the appropriate style given the followers and the situation; the leader's capacity to sharpen the skills necessary for guiding the self, the followers, and the organization toward advancement; and the leader's ability to remain emotionally attuned to the self, the stakeholders, and the environment, thereby maintaining the highest level of authenticity possible.

Because this definition is so wordy, let's reiterate the simplified version, along with the promised model.

An Awakened Leader is *a leader who is awake*. We refer not only to the literal sense of *awake*, but to every sense. An Awakened Leader maintains a high level of alertness in every regard:

- toward him- or herself and his or her driving motives in various matters;
- toward the people he or she guides;
- toward the organization he or she leads;
- toward the environment in which his or her organization operates;
- toward the entire universe.

Figure 1.1 illustrates the dimensions of Awakened Leadership as described above.

Figure 1.1: **Dimensions of Awakened Leadership**

Dimensions of Wakefulness

Another interesting way to look at the behavior of an Awakened Leader is through dimensions of wakefulness. Wakefulness can be segmented into many dimensions. For the purpose of conciseness, we'll only review three basic areas here: 1) internal wakefulness, 2) external wakefulness, and 3) integrated wakefulness. Each of these layers can, in turn, be subdivided further.

Internal Wakefulness

Internal wakefulness involves your connection with your center, your inner source of wisdom. It pertains to the awareness that all answers lie inside, and that you can only get to the answers if you're willing to listen to yourself.

Internal wakefulness can be subdivided into two main sections:

1) *Rational wakefulness*, which pertains to areas such as intellectual skills, ethical sense, and beliefs. When you get in touch with this part of your inner self, you review whether an action you're about to undertake is something you really want to do—and can do—given your skills, time, interests, and goals in life. You also review whether there could

be any ethical problem with the action to be undertaken: would it be okay if your loved ones knew about it? Would it be okay if it got published in tomorrow's newspaper? And then, if you feel that in your *own* realm of truth this act will be ethically sound, then you can proceed to the next step: Is this action you're about to undertake in line with your beliefs? Do you feel that there's a need for it? Will it add value to life? Is it in line with what you see as your purpose in life?

2) *Emotional wakefulness*, which touches on areas such as emotional intelligence, intuition, morals and values, self-perception, and passion. At this stage you dig even deeper, considering the impact of your action in the long term: Do you think you'll be able to look back at it some years from now and still be proud of it? How about those you care for—will they be proud of it, and will it provide them gratification as well? What does your gut feeling tell you about this act? Does it feel good, or do you have some vague doubts about its soundness? And even if your action may be ethically sound in the eyes of the government and other bystanders, how does it feel toward your own, innermost value system? What effect will this act have on your self-esteem, particularly in the long

run? And how about your passion? Do you really want to do this? Are you willing to dedicate time, effort, and whatever else it takes to make this work?

External Wakefulness

External wakefulness pertains to your awareness of the world around you. If you're a leader of an organization, this wakefulness involves not only the environment within the organization, but also the industry in which the organization operates as well as other industries your company might enter, and the world at large. The same principle goes for a family or any other group setting: you don't just consider the immediate environs, but the societal and global scope as well.

From the above we can conclude that external wakefulness can be subdivided into three basic segments:

1) *Close external wakefulness*, which pertains to your behavior within the organization (or family, or group) and the way you treat the people and processes around you. Elements such as continuous questioning of processes in order to establish an upward-spiraling learning climate belong to this area. In other words, you keep a close eye on potential

developments in your immediate environs at this level.

The way home furnishing retailer IKEA deals with employees' creativity is a good example of close external wakefulness. Workers enjoy great autonomy; their mistakes are reviewed as lessons to learn from and opportunities for growth. This attitude encourages initiative and ownership, and increases inventive behavior.

2) *Medial external wakefulness*, which involves skills such as developing vision for the organization or group, one or more strategies toward realizing the vision, and the continuous alertness necessary to analyze trends and use them to benefit the organization or group. As an Awakened Leader you'll most apparently use your wakefulness in this regard to alter the perceived trends in order to become the change agent in the organization's industry or in the group's environment.

   The way Southwest Airlines changed the face of traveling within the U.S. speaks volumes here. Focusing on a more pragmatic approach and implementing more lenient procedures regarding seating, flight attendants' behavior, and ticket options, this company has set new trends in its industry, remaining profitable as other companies face one crisis after another.

3) *Distant external wakefulness*, which pertains to global effects of the activities of the organization or group. Awakened Leaders will, at this level, consistently attempt to decrease harm done to various milieus and settings due to the activities of their organization. At the same time, they will attempt to increase advantages for as many and as wide a range of stakeholders as possible.

   Companies in the timber industry come to mind here. In South America, concessions are only given to those companies that agree to plant another tree for each one they cut. This commitment toward maintaining the "lungs of the world" isn't just an important rule for the local society, but guarantees health for the entire globe as well.

Integrated Wakefulness

Integrated wakefulness pertains to the way you intertwine your internal and external wakefulness attributes. It addresses how you integrate your values, intuition, emotional intelligence, knowledge, beliefs, ethics, self-perception, and passion with the given circumstances of the organization, its workers, its current direction, its potential, its industry including all stakeholders, and the world at large.

Integrated wakefulness is the most complicated part of being a leader because it pertains so much to action through perceived compatibility. If there's no compatibility between your internal qualities and your external environment, there will be no integration, only one of the two following options: 1) You'll exit the organization, or 2) the organization will undergo some sort of change in order to establish equilibrium between its operations and your perspectives.

Figure 1.2 illustrates the role that wakefulness plays in an Awakened Leader's life.

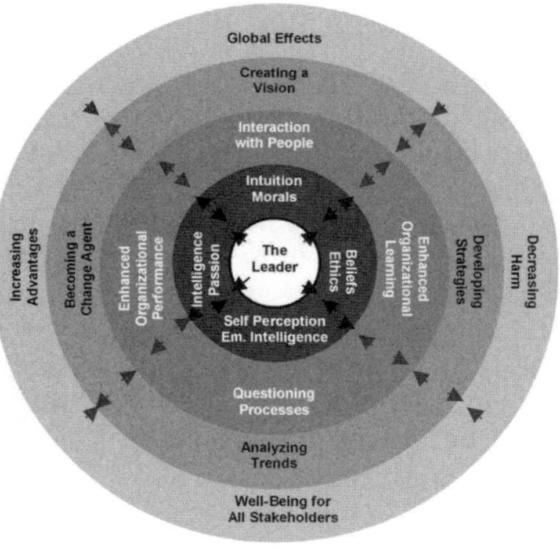

Figure 1.2: The Role of Wakefulness in an Awakened Leader's Organization

Endnote

It's important to keep in mind that Awakened Leaders, being human and thus receptive to changing circumstances, constantly change themselves. As a result, some of their internal pillars of wakefulness may be subject to change as well. Fortunately, these changes are seldom radical. Some events in the leader's personal or professional life, on the other hand, can have greater consequence such as death, birth, intense exposure to another culture, or a great loss affecting the business. In such cases, the leader will probably reevaluate his or her areas of wakefulness, and calibrate them again toward the changing external circumstances in order to determine the possibility of continued integrated wakefulness, altered integrated wakefulness, or separation.

Figure 1.3 illustrates the reevaluation process as described above:

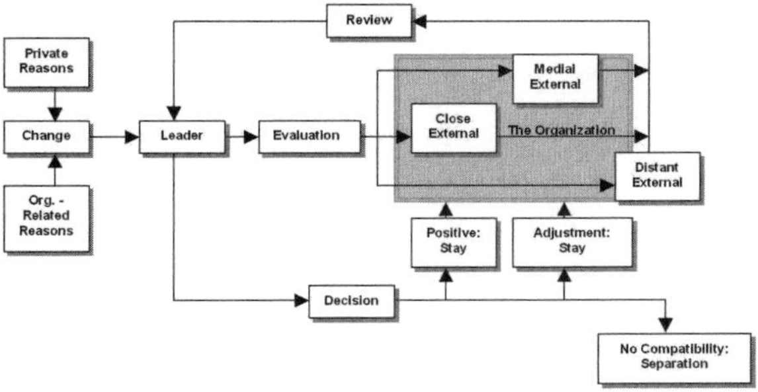

Figure 1.3: **The Reevaluation Dynamic in an Awakened Leader's Life**

In Review

This chapter introduced the concept of the Awakened Leader. Through a description of a meeting with an Awakened Leader and an overview of literature, we explored some of the familiar context of this type of leadership. The chapter reviewed Awakened Leadership from a hostorical as well as a contemporary perspective, then focused on the elements of Awakened Leadership, laying special emphasis on emotional intelligence and authenticity as pillars of this leadership style. The chapter also analyzed the concept of wakefulness, dividing it into three layers: internal, external, and integrated. Three models were presented to illustrate the theories introduced in the chapter.

Sources cited in Chapter 1:

- Bennis, W. (2003). Flight of the phoenix. *Executive Excellence, 20*(5), 4.
- Curtin, L. L. (1995). The "gold collar" leader...? *Nursing Management, 26*(10), 7-8.
- *Emotional intelligence*. (2006, Feb. 8). Wikipedia.org. Retrieved February 11, 2006, from http://en.wikipedia.org/wiki/Emotional_intelligence
- George, B. (2003). Authentic leadership. *CMA Management, 77*(8), 6.
- George, B. (2003). Taking charge: Vision and heart. *Chief Executive* (194), 30-32.
- Goleman, D. (1998). The emotionally competent leader. *The Healthcare Forum Journal, 42*(2), 36-38.
- Harung, H. S., Heaton, D. P., & Alexander, C. N. (1995). A unified theory of leadership: Experiences of higher states of consciousness in world-class leaders. *Leadership & Organization Development Journal, 16*(7), 44-59.
- Hughes, R. L., Ginnett, R. C., & Curphy, G. J. (2002). *Leadership: Enhancing the lessons of experience*. New York: McGraw-Hill.
- Kornfield, J. (1999). *Teachings of the Buddha*. Boston: Shambhala Publications.
- Madsen, S. R., & Hammond, S. C. (2005). Where have all the leaders gone? An interview with Margaret J. Wheatley on life-affirming leadership. *Journal of Management Inquiry, 14*(1), 71-77.
- Mayer, J. D., Caruso, D. R., & Salovey, P. (1999). Emotional intelligence meets traditional standards for an intelligence. *Intelligence, 27*(4), 267.
- Northouse, P. G. (2000). *Leadership theory and practice*. Thousand Oaks: Sage Publications.
- Pierce, J. L., & Newstrom, J. W. (2003). *Leaders and the leadership process*. New York: McGraw Hill.
- Secretan, L. (2001). The conscious leader. *Industry Week, 250*(2), 19-20.
- *Servant Leadership*. (2006, Feb 8). Wikipedia.org. Retrieved February 11, 2006, from http://en.wikipedia.org/wiki/Servant_leadership

These are some points I want to remember from this chapter:
My personal opinions after reading this chapter:

Chapter 2: Traits of an Awakened Leader

A real leader faces the music,
even when he doesn't like the tune.
Author Unknown

What's Ahead

In this chapter we'll zoom in a bit more extensively on some of the traits you'll typically encounter in Awakened Leaders. These are traits that you'll want to further develop if you're attracted to the idea of becoming an Awakened Leader. The list is by no means exhaustive, but it will serve to round out the character of this type of person.

An Awakened Leader is driven by more than organizational objectives

Even if you've obtained your leadership position on the basis of your outstanding qualities, you should also keep in mind who drives the organization: the people. You should therefore ensure that everyone involved is treated well: workers at all levels, shareholders, suppliers, customers, neighbors, and all others at stake. As an Awakened Leader you should ensure that the objectives of your organization are aligned to the well-being of the people who make it what it is. And you should keep them abreast of trends that the organization follows.

You should also consider the physical environment that hosts your organization. Being highly aware of the importance of life as a gift to all the living, you should refrain from setting organizational objectives that can be hazardous to the quality of life. If there are processes within the organization that form potential hazards to health, you should search for alternatives to these processes that will protect the quality of life everywhere.

An Awakened Leader is value-based

As an Awakened Leader you largely base your decisions on values. Values are the personal rules you develop as you grow up. They come from home, school, religion, books, and other sources throughout your life. Values therefore differ from person to person, from culture to culture, and from background to background.

Does this mean that an Awakened Leader in the U.S. will probably make different decisions from an Awakened Leader in, say, Japan? Perhaps. In fact, we don't even have to go that far away: two Awakened Leaders on the same street can make entirely different decisions. And, by the same token, two Awakened Leaders from entirely diverging cultures can make a similar decision!

The basic premise is that there's no single way of leading that's far and away more effective than another; diverging decisions can all lead to useful outcomes. It's not necessarily the nature of a decision, but rather the actions undertaken after the decision has been made, that determines its success.

As an Awakened Leader you should be aware that, regardless of your good intentions, things could go wrong. And that's okay, as long as the intentions are good, lessons are learned, and damage is kept to a minimum.

In sum, as an Awakened Leader you base your decisions on facts, knowledge, previous experiences, counsel from trusted sources, and the guidance of your intuition that derives from your values. Why? Because you should attempt at all times to stay in touch with your inner self. So, if a certain act is legally sound, yet morally unjust, you should seek alternatives.

The strength of leading on the basis of values and being awake at the same time lies in the fact that you're not blind to options, and you know they'll appear when you least expect them. If that sounds a little too romantic for a leader in today's die-hard world, then ask some of the great leaders you know and admire how often they ultimately made a decision on the basis of a prayer or a bright insight they got at the eleventh hour, one in line with their values.

An interesting example of a timely decision based on values and wakefulness can be found in the action of Doug Durand. Doug, who had worked for many years in the pharmaceutical industry, joined TAP Pharmaceutical Products, Inc. in 1995. He soon learned that bribery, overcharging, and other unlawful practices had long contributed to the company's financial success. Moreover, these practices were ongoing and considered "business as usual"! Providing freebies to urologists and the media in return for favors was a regular subject in the staff's conversations.

Durand made a decision on the basis of his values: he secretly started taping these conversations and made copies of documents proving the company's abusive practices. Although he realized the risks of being a whistle-blower (such as never finding a job again), he was much more troubled by the prospect of acquiescing to the company's unethical practices.

Durand sued TAP and earned more than $70 million for his efforts—a handsome reward for a conscious and courageous decision to act on his moral values.

An Awakened Leader has a high degree of integrity

Integrity goes hand in hand with trustworthiness and honesty, doesn't it? Well, as an Awakened Leader you know how important it is that your followers believe in you. That's why you should always speak and encourage the truth, even when it doesn't sound as beautiful as you'd wish.

Truthful communication is crucial. If you inform people about what's going on, they'll be more understanding, and consequently, more willing to do whatever it takes to get things straight.

When you ask anyone what qualities they like to see in their leader, integrity will invariably land somewhere in the top five of the list. As working adults we all know that it's not always pleasant to hear the truth. But it's better to deal with the truth now than a beautiful lie that causes more headache and pain later.

That's one of the reasons Awakened Leaders opt for integrity: People appreciate knowing what's going on rather than figuring out the truth behind concealed facts.

The other reason you should choose integrity is for the sake of your own inner peace.

Inner peace is only possible when you're truthful with yourself, as the above example of Doug Durand demonstrates.

As an Awakened Leader, you reflect integrity not only in your communication with stakeholders, but also in the way you guide the organization. Involvement in questionable practices is taboo, even if the organization's future existence seems to depend on it—"seems to," I say, because as an Awakened Leader you should maintain the conviction that, with the right intentions, it is very likely that a better option will surface, allowing the organization to maintain a trustworthy image.

An Awakened Leader has genuine compassion and respect for those he or she leads

If you're an Awakened Leader, you're down to earth with respect to every member of your organization. Everything and everybody has equal importance to the performance of the business.

You should therefore make it a point to mingle with your employees on a regular basis in order to establish a connection, because connectivity is what creates goodwill and support in all directions. However, you shouldn't only mingle with your employees because it motivates them to perform better, but more so because you have a quest for learning, and you realize that teachers appear at the most unexpected moments and in the most unexpected places. As an Awakened Leader you should maintain your readiness to learn from every person you encounter in the organization. Rather than treating co-workers as means toward an end, treat them as ends unto themselves.

Awakened Leaders' compassion is expressed through their availability and listening skills. Again, communication is critical here: you should regularly give co-workers the opportunity to express themselves and be incorporated into the big picture.

When a co-worker meets with you, don't just listen with your ears, but with your heart and mind as well. The unspoken should also be heard, which means that you should pay attention to the body language of the other person. If you do that, the co-worker will sense that you're truly giving your full attention.

As an Awakened Leader you should further ensure that compassion and respect are maintained throughout the organization. You can't possibly be the only one executing these qualities. That's why you need to communicate the essence of respect and compassion at every opportunity. That's also why you should try to ensure, particularly in the hiring process of managers, that they harbor these qualities.

If you find that there are members in the organization who attempt to build fiefdoms, you should communicate your concern to these hierarchy-addicts and try to guide them toward improvement. If, after appropriate guidance and repeated communication, they fail to adjust this poisonous attitude, you should release them in favor of the well-being of the organization.

An Awakened Leader touches the spirit of the people in the organization

As an Awakened Leader you should go to great lengths (but still within consideration of your values) to provide a sense of meaning to the people in your organization. Plan update sessions, company gatherings, and family days. Enable regular lines of communication through email, flyers, or departmental meetings in order to continue encouraging your co-workers.

You could consider meetings in which groups have the opportunity to ask questions. At Cisco Systems employees are encouraged to present questions to the CEO in the monthly staff meeting in their birthday month. Of course there are alternative means of giving everybody a chance to voice questions, opinions, or concerns, such as arranging people alphabetically.

You should also bear in mind that the people working in your organization have families, and therefore, lives with hobbies and skills independent of the organization. Encourage them to share those skills and hobbies with others. You might consider art or music events to showcase the skills and talents of co-workers and their family members.

Encourage your workers to display family pictures and drawings from the kids to help create a pleasant atmosphere in the workplace. After all, who would mind seeing a cute drawing from a child on the wall of an office? Doesn't that create a sense of informality, comfort, and plain humanity?

The message is clear: the entire organization benefits when you recognize workers as spiritual beings with various responsibilities and qualities that exist beyond the scope of their organizational roles. You should value the aspects of co-workers that make them well-rounded, unique, and whole individuals by encouraging them to cultivate and develop their good qualities.

Awakened Leaders ensure that their mission at work is connected with their mission as human beings

This quality is similar to the value base discussed above. Indeed, there are many connection points here. But this characteristic of an Awakened Leader does not only pertain to his or her values; it reaches a bit further. Consider it this way:

We all have a mission, and it's very instructive to formulate your mission statement. If you've never done so, you might want to consider writing it down now. It's a great exercise in finding out what your current focus is in life. It's also important to realize that your mission can change over time; however, there will be some basics incorporated in your life's mission that will remain constant.

As an Awakened Leader you should know your mission and keep it in mind in every major act that you perform such as accepting a leadership position in an organization. If the organization's product or service line isn't congruent with your mission, you shouldn't accept the position. If the organization's business strategy isn't in line with your mission, you should either enter the environment with the intent to change it as soon as possible, or forego the position. And if the members of the organization are known as extremely aggressive, petty, backstabbing, and uncooperative, you should consider whether it's worth your while to attempt a change or to enter the organization in the first place.

Don't allow yourself to worry about others seeing you as a quitter, particularly when it pertains to stepping out of an environment that's persistently toxic. Because of your connection with your inner self, you should sense when a challenge is worthwhile and when it isn't.

An example of an appealing company mission statement is the one from Amazon.com: "Our mission is to use the Internet to offer products that educate, inform, and inspire. We decided to build an online store that would be customer-friendly and easy to navigate and would offer the broadest possible selection."

In this statement, Jeff Bezos, founder and CEO of Amazon.com, expresses the things he considers most important for his organization: education, inspiration, people-friendliness, accessibility, and assortment.

An Awakened Leader tends to be:

- ***Warm, yet challenging***

An example may be the best way to describe this quality: When I served as an academic advisor at a university in Burbank, California, one of the department chairs with whom I had a close relationship would regularly approach me with projects that he needed assistance with. Although the projects were not part of my assigned duties, his humble way of bringing up the issue, along with his enthusiastic way of "selling" his case, worked like a charm. Every time. This leader had a warm way about him—an inspirational way—that easily got me interested and involved in his projects. More importantly, he gave me co-ownership in them, granting me the recognition he thought I deserved when his projects were ready for presentation. Even in the follow-up stages, he ensured that my involvement was given credit and rewarded. The projects usually weren't the easiest jobs to execute; they required days, sometimes weeks of stressful time in front of the computer to achieve the right format and proper representation of his views. It was extremely challenging, but knowing for whom I did it and why I did it were two fabulous drivers to keep me going. The insight that these projects gave me added meaning to our mutual work environment and were of tremendous value.

- ***Inspired, yet practical***

Since we're on an example spree here, let's continue: At another time in the same work environment, I was working closely with the Dean of the School of Business. One of the MBA students suggested starting a career service center geared toward the MBA student population. Great idea! The Dean established contact between the student and me, and based on this student's ideas I developed a structure and action plan for a new departmental program. Once that was established, the Dean and I lobbied for the creation and funding of this center, each at our own level: I approached the Student Association; he contacted the Board of Trustees. I remember very well the opposition we faced while developing this project; every reason in the world why this MBA Career Center would not fly was brought up. But the Dean was inspired and believed in the purpose of this project, and so did I. We systematically tackled each hurdle until there was none left, and the Center has been up and running for six years.

- ***Capable of balancing the economic needs of the business with the human needs***

This capability brings to mind a non-profit entity that I worked with a number of years ago. Somewhere along the line funding got scarce, and the CEO knew he would have to come up with an ingenious idea to obtain funds to keep it running. Scanning the available options, he zeroed in on a graffiti awareness project for elementary schools that was sponsored by the City of Los Angeles. He recruited me to coordinate and execute the project, which emerged as a great success seen from multiple angles: 1) it gave the organization an ensured source of income; 2) it provided a number of employees a steady job and a decent paycheck to support their families; and 3) it educated the youth in the community about the negative consequences of vandalism and the positive results of beautification and maintenance. Economic needs and human needs could not have been more closely aligned.

An Awakened Leader responds to a deep-rooted calling to make a difference in the world

What better names come to mind here than Nelson Mandela, Mahatma Gandhi, Martin Luther King Jr., Mother Teresa, and, further back in time, Siddhartha Gautama (Buddha) and Jesus Christ? Although one may dispute whether all of these leaders were Awakened Leaders in every sense of the word, they all definitely responded to that calling! Their contributions to change in the world are undisputable.

Yet, even at less visible and imposing levels it is entirely possible to make a difference in the world. If Confucius' concept of a better world starting with only two people and the concept of a tornado starting with the mere flutter of a butterfly's wings are true (and why wouldn't they be?), then the philosophy should also hold that making a difference in the world starts with establishing positive change at the micro level, shouldn't it?

Being an Awakened Leader means being aware of a calling to make a difference, and keeping this purpose in mind all the time. What does it matter if you never make it to Oprah or Larry King with your project? What does it matter that no one will write a book about your contribution toward a positive difference in the world? Let's be realistic: What really matters in "doing well by doing good" isn't that you win a Nobel Prize or world fame, but that you obtain a tremendous intrinsic reward from these actions through feeling good about what you do. What is more beautiful than looking in the eyes of a person whom you helped in ways that you never could have imagined? What is more rewarding than knowing that one good cause was served because of your intervention? Whether it pertains to the loving upbringing of your children, tender care for aged parents, warm attention for a lonely neighbor, filling in for a colleague in trouble, going an extra mile for an employee in need, or developing a new product or an entire industry to the benefit of millions of lives—the inner gratification is similar. And so is the appreciation from the universe.

Awakened Leaders have the ability to reach beyond themselves for something higher and more meaningful

One thing that you should realize as an Awakened Leader is that the main purpose of living isn't to make a lot of money, but to leave a legacy. Like Stephen R. Covey worded it in Habit 4 of his book *The Seven Habits of Highly Effective People*: "Begin with the end in mind. Well, you may not want to think of your funeral (who wants to?), but you should definitely keep in mind that there's more to life than just material affluence."

Although you, as an Awakened Leader, are down to earth, or perhaps *because* of that, you should reach beyond just a fat paycheck. You should realize that *success* doesn't always mean material abundance, but that it has much more to do with doing the right thing. Success, for an Awakened Leader, has everything to do with a sense of contentment and fulfillment in life. So, as an Awakened Leader, you should continuously strive toward bringing meaning into your life, and into the lives of those you deal with, whether in the workplace or elsewhere.

An interesting discovery that you'll make is that once you do what you like best, rewards will automatically follow. It may take time before you reap material rewards from doing what you enjoy (particularly because it may not be obvious immediately *what* you really do like most), but once you've figured that out and have determined your purpose, the rest will be relatively easy.

The whole point here is that you should refrain from being absorbed by what seems to have become the rule of life in today's corporate world: infinitely greater return on investment for yourself and for your organization at any cost. That's what makes you different from others; that's why you are *awake*. You woke up from that nightmare and saw the light, the real purpose of it all: enjoying what you are doing here by making sure that others enjoy the ride as well. It's important, also, to align activities in a way that the cost of living can be covered and the organization, as the *home away from home,* can grow. Thus, we can continue to generate our livelihood while being proud of what we're doing.

An Awakened Leader is in essence a servant leader

One of the leaders I interviewed for this book offered this insightful comment: "I think servant leadership and Awakened Leadership go hand in hand. Now, one could be a servant leader without being an Awakened Leader, probably, but I think an Awakened Leader should always have that quality of wanting to serve others, and understand that the concept of leadership is service and not domination."

I think the above statement was very well expressed. It isn't always easy to think of a leader in a die-hard business environment as a servant leader, because the term *servant leader* may bring up the image of a person who walks around all day long with his or her hands crossed behind the back, asking everybody how he or she can serve them. That's not exactly what a servant leader is about, and surely not what an Awakened Leader is about. Serving is possible without sacrificing one's dignity and influence.

Serving, in this regard, should be seen in a much broader light: serving the organization, and therefore the well-being of all those affected by its existence. If we look at it that way, we can see a full-time job emerging. We can envision a combination of internal and external practices that fill the plate of the Awakened Leader. We can envision time scheduled for taking care of internal matters of the organization, listening to employees, and scanning the market in order to see how the organization can get ahead in a fair manner within its industry. We can also see time allotted for adjusting the organization's vision to economic changes or a change in goals.

We can also envision time allotted to the leader's personal well-being. That, too, is part of serving: serving your health and emotional condition in order to continue doing the right thing without overworking. Overwork reduces the sense of enjoyment you can have from doing what you like best.

Awakened Leaders create time to examine their nature, goals, and actions

Although we touched on the leader's search for meaning above, the topic bears further discussion from the most subjective point of view: While an Awakened Leader will search for meaning and find it when awakened, it's also important to answer the question, "Who am I?"

Many philosophers will tell us that it is practically impossible to know who we really are, in that the search is almost a full-time job. But as an Awakened Leader, being practical enough to know when things become compulsive, you'll likely only go far enough to be able to formulate what you like or dislike, what makes you happy or sad, and what really "stokes your fire." It's up to you if you want to take it a tad further, but for the initial stage of being in touch with yourself, these three points are sufficient.

- Knowing what you like or dislike helps you determine which directions to go with your life and which to avoid.

- Knowing what makes you happy and sad helps you determine your definition of contentment and success, and helps you decide what you want to work on.

- Knowing what moves you to act helps you formulate your vision in life, and as a result, your mission, with the realization that visions and missions may change over time as life circumstances change. Knowing what really motivates you will thus help you formulate what you want to accomplish in life, and subsequently, a strategy to get there.

Awakened Leaders sense the greatness lying within the heart and soul of every person they meet

To some this trait may sound gullible, but it isn't. It just indicates that you should maintain a positive mindset and be willing to give everybody a fair chance. It also indicates that you shouldn't judge a person solely on the basis of his or her reputation, being aware of human nature and the inclination of some people to blackball others. As an Awakened Leader, you should refrain from branding or labeling a person based on a reputation or initial impression. This quality evolves with time and through life experience. That's why an Awakened Leader is often one who has known the injustice of being unfairly judged and deprived of opportunity based on misrepresentation from others.

Once you're awakened, you'll feel the greatness within the heart and soul of every person you meet. This is the beauty of being awakened: *You'll always attempt to meet the greatness you perceive in others, rather than their peripheral ranks and societal labels*. You'll try to connect with their greatness and learn from it every time you meet them. Each encounter in your life should lead to self-reflection, adopting the positive lessons learned from others, and sharpening your emotional intelligence, which is expressed through self-knowledge and knowledge of others.

As the above suggests, being able to see or feel the greatness in everyone you encounter also confronts you with your own flaws, inspiring you to continue working on them. It keeps you humble and encourages you to continuously strive for betterment.

As an Awakened Leader you should never be destructive to yourself or others. If you perceive a great skill or quality in another person, you shouldn't become jealous or envious, but rather try to match the other's strength by exerting great efforts to better yourself. You learn from others through the spoken and the unspoken word, as well as through reflection.

An Awakened Leader is compassionate and passionate

These two terms sound alike, yet they can complement each other or conflict. As an Awakened Leader you should use these two qualities in the complementary sense: You should be compassionate toward humanity, yet your compassion should extend to all forms of life. While you guard this quality as a valuable trait, you shouldn't deprive yourself from the firmness and decisiveness of a leader. Nevertheless, your sensitivity reaches beyond empathy for human beings. You have great respect for everything that lives or once lived, and you recognize a teacher in all. This is the compassionate part.

As for passion, you should engage in everything with the greatest enthusiasm and devotion. An important trait of an Awakened Leader is that he or she always wants to do everything well. An Awakened Leader is far from ignorant and takes responsibility seriously, whether it's leading the organization, guiding the people, formulating the vision and the mission, contemplating on new directions, or devoting yourself to family life and other social callings without drowning in the multiplicity of life. You are passionate about your duties because you perceive them as opportunities to live life to the fullest.

As an Awakened Leader you'll be cautious about passion, though, and disallow this emotion to cause you problems. Guided by your values, vision, mission, and continuous search for meaning, you should use passion to complement compassion rather than undercut it.

An Awakened Leader has vision

The first important note to make here is that there's nothing wrong with dreaming big—not even when you're awake. Actually, *because* you are awake, you should dare to dream. However, your dream shouldn't become an obsession, and should be subject to change if circumstances warrant it. But it's important to have a vision, not only for the organization you lead, but also for yourself. It is this vision that leads you through life.

Because visions are long-term goals, you should carefully lay out your vision and think of alternative strategies to realize it. At the same time, you should remember that everything in life is subject to change, so keep in mind that your vision may have to change as well. Here's where you'll benefit from your wakefulness: As an Awakened Leader, you're fully aware of the inconsistency of life and the insecurity of everything. Thus, you won't be crushed when your vision needs to be modified. You're aware of alternatives to your vision, and you remain alert for internal and external developments in order to add new visions to existing ones.

An Awakened Leader sees the whole, yet values the individual parts as well

Here's where the dual-perception ability of an Awakened Leader comes in handy: You should develop an eye for the big picture, which is like knowing whether the team is still operating in the right forest, but at the same time you should keep an eye on the details, which is like knowing which trees to cut in order to get the best results. Not to forget, you should also nurture the good trees and plant new ones in order to keep the forest in existence.

This quality of seeing the whole as well as the individual parts isn't just limited to processes and strategies. You can apply this combined holistic-individual awareness toward all constituencies, particularly those you work with. It should be possible for you to see the value of the entire organization including its diversity of characters, skills, ages, ethnicities, and perceptions, while you also appreciate every single worker.

The Macro-to-Micro Paradigm:
An Awakened Leader makes decisions from a global perspective, with individuals in mind

While the topic of this section is closely related to the previous one, there's an important shift in perspective here. We're now talking about operating on an inter-city, inter-state, or international level. Awakened Leaders, especially those who operate in multiple cultures, should be aware of the need to implement two important strategies: 1) thinking globally, acting locally; and 2) thinking locally, acting locally.

In the first perspective, you should maintain close awareness of trends that occur in the larger perspective (within your industry and outside of it) in order to apply changes when necessary, while you should also engage in attuning the organization's productions and behavior to the local culture.

In the second perspective, you should ensure at a deeper level that the localness of the organization is fully established and understood by all stakeholders, and that employees at all levels in the organization are aware of the importance of making this particular branch fit into the local society. This is where you should ensure that the leaders of such a branch are good citizens, engaging in activities that enhance the quality of life in the local community. That's what thinking and acting locally is all about. This perspective also elicits the paradigm of making decisions from a global perspective in consideration of the individuals involved.

An Awakened Leader holds to specific theories

1. Awakened Leaders believe in loving what they do in order to make it a success. They take pride in what they do. Awakened Leaders love their job, and they positively influence their environment with this attitude.

2. Awakened Leaders are very relationship-oriented without losing sight of the production process or the return on investment. Rather, by establishing a great connection with their co-workers they manage to create a workplace with satisfied people and, consequently, optimal output.

3. Awakened Leaders understand the value of earning money, but they don't prioritize it over all else. Rather, they realize that earnings will be a logical consequence of the above two points: loving the job and loving the people.

An Awakened Leader holds to high standards

An Awakened Leader works hard and expects the same from co-workers. Yet, at the same time the leader understands the value of family and leisure, so he or she encourages employees to balance their lives in a gratifying way. The leader strives to do the same.

Awakened Leaders are honest and generous, and expect the same from their co-workers in order to keep the environment from becoming toxic.

An Awakened Leader prefers clarity

This can be interpreted in different ways: First, *you* communicate. Everything. All the time. You do this because you understand the importance of keeping people informed about your decisions. Second, you encourage communication *from all sides*. For this reason, you advocate an open-door policy and the prevention of useless hierarchal hurdles.

Aside from using clarity in communication, you should also use it in the sense of honesty. Honesty is clarity on a different level. In sum, you should promote honest communication—not internal marketing babble to keep people satisfied, but a continuous flow of the bare-bone facts. Adults appreciate that.

An Awakened Leader would do no deliberate harm

Some caution is required here: Although Awakened Leaders may never have the intention to do anyone harm, there will be times that such cannot be prevented. Having to lay off people is sometimes inevitable, even when we know that these employees have families and that their livelihood is brought into jeopardy. Therefore, whenever a lay off is imminent, an Awakened Leader will do two things:

1) communicate the reasons for the pending lay off candidly;
2) facilitate retraining programs for these workers, so they can readily gain reemployment.

The Awakened Leader will also ensure that workers are released with dignity, and that they get all the support the organization and its management can afford to reinvent themselves and move on. This explains why individuals who are laid off in organizations where there's Awakened Leadership will always attempt to return when the tide turns.

There are, of course, other areas in which Awakened Leaders could do harm, even unintentionally. Sometimes getting ahead in the business world happens at the expense of other organizations, in bidding processes for instance. If the organization led by the Awakened Leader wins the bid, this automatically means that other organizations lose, with all possible consequences for their workers. However, it needs to be reemphasized that an Awakened Leader won't harm anyone deliberately, and will always opt for the win-win-win perspective: benefit for all parties involved, as well as for the environment.

In Review

This chapter presented a number of typical traits that Awakened Leaders nurture. Some of these traits were:

- Drive
- Value Base
- Integrity
- Compassion and Respect
- Spiritual Connection
- Mission
- Broad-Mindedness
- Focus on Meaning
- Serving Mentality
- Goals
- Actions
- Perceptiveness
- Passion
- Vision
- Orientation to Detail
- Standards
- Clarity
- Harm Aversion

These are some points I want to remember from this chapter:
My personal opinions after reading this chapter:

Chapter 3:

Awakened Leaders: Born or Made?

I have three precious things, which I hold fast and prize. The first is gentleness; the second is frugality; the third is humility, which keeps me from putting myself before others. Be gentle and you can be bold; be frugal and you can be liberal; avoid putting yourself before others and you can become a leader among men.

Lao-Tzu

What's Ahead

This chapter explains why Awakened Leaders are made and not born. The chapter reviews 21 trial-and-error areas that led to a leader's wakefulness. Although each point contains a short explanation, the final trial area, which is change, gets extensive reviewed due to its importance in today's fast-paced world.

An Awakened Leader is the one leader who was not born but made—made by life and made by the experiences he or she had while growing up. Although Awakened Leaders may have been born with certain skills that enhanced their chances and marked their aspirations toward becoming a leader, they were ultimately made by *trial and error*.

In many serious environments the trial and error phenomenon is a red flag because it indicates a waste of time, money, energy, and prestige. But the making of an Awakened Leader cannot happen in any other way than by trial and error, so maybe this is one of the rare circumstances where the phenomenon should be considered a good one.

Many Awakened Leaders have made their share of mistakes and have experienced some pretty humbling situations. But that's exactly what makes them such bright persons today: they were sleepwalking through life (like we all do at one time or another), when something happened to wake them up. And it is exactly due to their blunders in the past that Awakened Leaders are now such reliable, honest, fair, and flexible persons to work with: in short, such good role models.

So, what are some of the trials and errors that led to the awakening of such a leader?

- ***Morals and values:*** Awakened Leaders may have been confronted with issues that caused them to question their morals and reconsider them. Sometimes we have to be confronted with the opposite of our beliefs before we learn to respect other perspectives. The confrontation with mind-boggling circumstances teaches Awakened Leaders to understand different perspectives, and leads them to reevaluate and strengthen their own morals and values.

- ***Ethics:*** Ethics, like morals and values, are subjective perspectives, which are heavily culture-, environment-, and person-bound. Awakened Leaders are not spared from ethical dilemmas. Sometimes it is just this type of dilemma that causes a leader to become wakeful. It could be the case of a co-worker who gets fired due to unethical behavior. Or it could be a confrontation with two alternatives: one that's ethical but less profitable versus one that's highly profitable but unethical. Facing such issues usually strengthens Awakened Leaders in their ethical standpoints.

- ***Integrity, honesty, and trust:*** We all confront people who don't hold up their end of a bargain and damage our trust. Awakened Leaders have also experienced their share of these people. These confrontations taught them an important lesson: to keep *their* word when they give it. They know too well what it feels like to be disappointed by others' dishonest and untrustworthy behavior. And they learn from it.

- ***Vision:*** Either through reading, listening, or experiencing, Awakened Leaders have learned the importance of having vision. They have seen too many organizations floating along without a long-term perspective, or with one that's a hundred years old. They see promising mergers and acquisitions from gigantic companies go bad due to lack of vision and insufficient consideration of a strategy after the fusion. And they learn from that.

- ***Respect:*** In private as well as in professional situations, Awakened Leaders have learned the value of showing respect. They may have made their own share of mistakes in this regard as well. After all, once they were also young and rebellious and thought that nobody could teach them anything. But they woke up—oftentimes, through heartache and shame. Yet, they learned from it.

- ***Passion:*** It rarely happens that an Awakened Leader ends up being the CEO in the work environment where he or she started his or her career. And that's a good thing. We all need exposure to different environments to determine what we really want. Through the various work environments that Awakened Leaders attend on their way to wakefulness, they encounter people with various attitudes and perspectives. They learn to distinguish passionate workers from ever-dissatisfied ones. And they make up their minds about whose example they want to follow.

- ***Commitment:*** On their way to maturity, Awakened Leaders also encounter people who are committed to their goals, and others who just do what they have to for a paycheck. Awakened Leaders consider these extremes. Through their observations they learn that commitment is a great quality to have, as long as it doesn't turn into obsession. So they learn from that as well.

- ***Compassion:*** Awakened Leaders have also dealt with various levels of compassion. They've learned that overly compassionate people can fall prey to abuse, and may run into situations where all their time and energy gets absorbed by other people's problems. They've also learned that people who have no compassion at all are usually disliked and will not be supported when they need a helping hand. Awakened Leaders have seen these extremes and learned that a balance is crucial.

- ***Justice:*** There may have been pretty painful circumstances at the foundation for Awakened Leaders' sense of justice. Sometimes these circumstances may even pertain to family members. But they've learned, not without suffering, that justice should be done, even if it means punishing those they love most. Awakened Leaders know that it ultimately serves everybody's best interest when justice is done.

- ***Kindness:*** Whether it is through first-hand experience of being treated with arrogance, or through observing arrogance directed toward someone close, Awakened Leaders learn the value of kindness. Kindness can also be learned from a positive experience: we may have encountered a person who was kind to us when we needed it most. This may have opened our eyes to the value of being kind to others.

- ***Forgiveness:*** Throughout their lives, Awakened Leaders have also encountered forgiveness: from parents, siblings, children, spouses, friends, or colleagues. When a person has received forgiveness from another, he or she will understand how good it feels, what a humbling experience it is, and how it will make him or her strive to be much better than before. Awakened Leaders have learned that lesson.

- ***Courage:*** Without having learned this lesson, Awakened Leaders would probably not have become leaders. Living takes courage, and so does leading. Awakened Leaders have observed that nothing happens without someone being courageous enough to take a first step. Awakened Leaders have learned that they could be that person. They've also learned that courage doesn't always pay off in terms of material or financial turnout, but it always leads to an enrichment of experiences and insights. And they value that.

- ***Love:*** This lesson may be the most precious one of all. It's about the caring concern an individual develops through life, on the way toward Awakened Leadership. It involves empathy, understanding, and accepting. It also involves learning that diversity is good, and that the connection of people from different backgrounds and cultures ultimately brings about greater insights. The lesson of love involves knowing what the right thing is to do, and realizing that differences among people were created for a purpose. Awakened Leaders have therefore learned to love people from all walks of life equally, and to respect them equally even if they don't always understand these people. They seek to understand, even if it takes time. Thus, Awakened Leaders have learned the essence of love.

- ***Deep listening:*** On our way through life we learn that there's a difference between hearing and listening, and between shallow listening and deep listening. Awakened Leaders have learned that people greatly appreciate it when they're listened to with more than just the leader's ears. Awakened Leaders may have learned this when *they* were listened to with more than ears alone. So they have learned to focus on others and listen deeply. And it has contributed to their awakening.

- ***Inspired and inspiring:*** Through life, Awakened Leaders have obtained inspiration from various sources. No one develops special skills without inspiration. This inspiration can come from other human beings, but also from other living entities such as animals or plants, or nature in its entirety. Awakened Leaders have learned from the various sources of inspiration they encountered through life. One of the most important overarching lessons Awakened Leaders have learned in this regard is that it is crucial to have a source of inspiration. So, now that they're awake, they do their utmost to become a source of inspiration to others as well. If you practice Awakened Leadership, you'll radiate it through your way of communicating with others, through the time you take to listen, to encourage, to provide guidelines, and to be available when needed. The inspired leader knows first and foremost the essence of being available. Because you've been there, you know that people sometimes just need an open ear for their issues, as most of the time they already know the answer. All they need is to hear themselves formulating it. By listening, you enable that process to happen. And don't think that Awakened Leaders don't need continued inspiration—they do. But they know by now where to get it. They open themselves to others and to experiences, and they have a frame of mind that absorbs everything in a constructive way. So they learn and derive inspiration from sources that may not be inspirational to others. They can get inspired by the simplest things, because they have an open mind; they try to perceive matters with an unlearned attitude, not with preconceived opinions, but with openness. This is the cycle of being inspired and serving as an inspiration at the same time. Awakened Leaders understand and practice that.

- ***Authenticity:*** As was mentioned above in Chapter 1, Awakened Leaders definitely practice authenticity, all the time. They've learned that it's too much hassle to put on different hats under different circumstances and to play different roles in front of different audiences. Mark Twain once said that if you always tell the truth, you don't have to remember. As an Awakened Leader you are aware of that and you live by it. You'll refrain from adopting shifting attitudes and behaviors, because you realize that there are more important things in life than putting up fronts. And that's the power of authenticity: honesty and straightforwardness that translate to others as simplicity, the way of being uncomplicated. And what is more rewarding than being valued for your simplicity? No one has to worry about your hidden intentions: everyone knows where they stand with you. That's what being an Awakened Leader is all about.

- ***Spiritual Connection:*** Awakened Leaders know that it is important to allocate time daily for contemplation; for turning to the source of wealth and knowledge within in search of answers. Awakened Leaders have learned that, by doing so frequently, they gain easier and quicker access to that connection with themselves. It's all about becoming familiar with the self. That's what Awakened Leaders do. This isn't to say that you are all religious people. Awakened Leaders can be found among people from various religions, and among people who don't follow any religion. Spirituality isn't a religion. It is the connection with your inner self that helps you formulate who you are, and helps you know your strengths and weaknesses, likes and dislikes, and the boundaries of your acceptance.

- ***Multidimensional:*** Awakened Leaders have learned to see things in different dimensions, and they make their decisions accordingly. They know from experience that, if they allow themselves to be driven by the right causes, rewards will follow. They're therefore never primarily money-driven. They know that the bottom line will be served in much more rewarding ways if the people and the relationships are nurtured. Awakened Leaders are relationship oriented, *first* because they like developing relationships and know the mutual value of maintaining them; and *second* because they know how important good relationships are for the advancement of their organization.

- ***Fulfillment:*** Trial and error in life is definitely the source of knowledge when it comes to fulfillment for Awakened Leaders. These leaders have learned that there's no gratification in material and financial affluence without fulfillment. They reflect on that experience toward themselves as well as those they surround themselves with. They strive in the first place for everyone to have a sense of fulfillment with what they do. And, as stated above, they know that financial and material rewards will follow once a person is doing the thing he or she gets a sense of fulfillment from. So fulfillment is very high on the agenda of an Awakened Leader.

- ***Initiative:*** Awakened Leaders have learned that nothing comes from waiting for others. So they take the initiative. Along with that, they're aware that not all initiatives work out. But they're still willing to go for it, because they perceive failed initiatives as life lessons. They pursue what they believe in, even if it takes a while to obtain it. They develop creativeness to get there. And they usually get there.

- ***Change:*** Awakened Leaders have learned through many experiences that no one can survive in today's world without being open to change, because changes are continuously brought upon us. Awakened Leaders have also learned that the most effective way to deal with change is to be just one step ahead, reinventing themselves on a regular basis. How? By keeping track of developments in their interest areas; by adopting a pro-learning mindset; and by refusing to let setbacks get the best of them. Awakened Leaders know that setbacks occur in everyone's life, but it's the perennial losers who dwell on them, while the winners look for the lessons to be learned from these setbacks and the opportunities hidden within or behind them.

Thus, Awakened Leaders will develop a plan to keep themselves at the forefront. How? There are several strategies that can be developed, and the following cycle called C H A N G E may become part of the Awakened Leader's regular routine. If you aspire to Awakened Leadership, keep these notes at hand so you can regularly review the cycle and get re-inspired.

Cycle of C H A N G E:

Check it out. The Internet, magazines, mentors, television, colleagues, and children—these are just a few of the numerous sources available to generate fresh ideas on how to keep yourself up-to-date. It all starts with a mindset that's geared toward learning: a hungry mind. Checking things out with a hungry mind, diligently seeking opportunities and ideas, will lead you to see more than you did before. You'll start thinking about things at a different level; you'll absorb information provided by friends, colleagues, and mentors in a more constructive way. You'll find that children's perspectives are not that silly at all. You'll come to view media sources as more than just passive ways of spending time; indeed, you'll start a continuous scanning process that will help you to break barriers, obtain ideas, formulate your vision, and find ways to realize it. And that's exactly what an Awakened Leader does!

Hash it over. Once you decided what your next move should be, discuss it with others whose opinions you value. Avoid naysayers, because they'll present all kinds of reasons why you won't be able to realize your vision. Instead, seek out the constructive souls, people who dare in a responsible way, people who also belong to the club of self-reinventors; you know who they are because their lives are proof of it.

Analyze. Here's where you start working on a strategy to go from where you are now, Point A, to where you want to be, Point B. Point of caution: keep it realistic, and be flexible. You may have to adjust your strategy toward reaching your goal more than once. Yet, once you've determined where you want to go, you'll need to know where you currently stand. Analyze your current circumstances. What does your point A look like? And what do you need to do to get to point B? Which skills do you need to upgrade? Here's a suggestion: Make a SWOT analysis of your status quo, whether it's a career-related or private goal you're after. As you may already know, SWOT stands for Strengths, Weaknesses, Opportunities, and Threats. The former two, strengths and weaknesses, are the internal issues you should work on; the latter two, opportunities and threats, are the external factors you may have to tackle.

Navigate: As a result of your self-evaluation, you can now start looking for ways to upgrade your skills in order to reinvent yourself. Oftentimes you'll need additional education. Find out what's available out there: schools, self-education tools (specialized books or magazines), or maybe even some traveling in order to acquire insight into other cultures and practices.

Get going: Start the upgrading process as soon as you've figured out what you need to do in order to achieve your goal. If it's formal education, enroll! If it's self-education, purchase the materials! Put your heart and soul into it, and don't give up when it becomes a bit difficult. Hardly anything gets achieved overnight. Besides, it feels so much better when you can look back and see how far you've come from the moment you acquired your idea for a new direction to the moment you've succeeded in your self-renewal process.

Execute! The final step is the most exciting and daring one. Here's where you finally make the leap toward the next phase in your life. Whether it's the move to a new job, the start up of your own business, or the initiation of a new love life: it is time for implementation.

You should also know that, aside from the above cycle, there are two crucial points to ponder:

1. All through the implementation of C H A N G E, you should keep scanning for opportunities, and for possible needs to adjust your direction.

2. Learning is never wasted. Even if, at the eleventh hour, you have to change your goal, you'll always be able to apply the lessons you've learned in some way or another. Don't get discouraged.

If you aspire to be an Awakened Leader, you should know that C H A N G E can be a lifesaver, especially if you get used to applying it on a regular basis. Cycles such as the one described above may save you from getting suffocated in the status quo. These cycles make life more exciting and rewarding, while they also enable you to adapt faster than others when surprises hit, because guess what? You were prepared!

Figure 3.1 illustrates the C H A N G E cycle as described above.

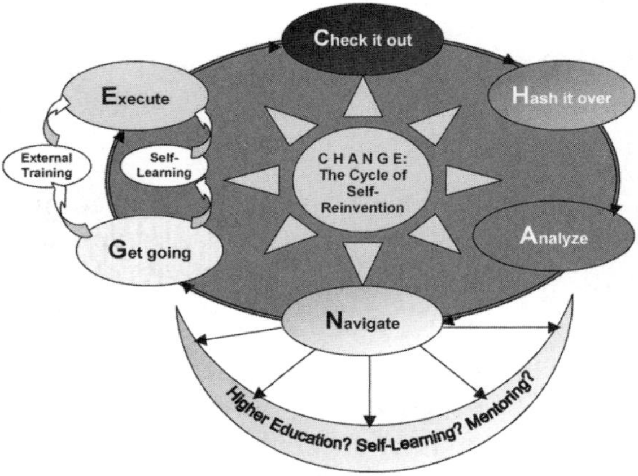

Figure 3.1: The C H A N G E Cycle of Self-Reinvention

In Review

In this chapter we listed 21 areas through which Awakened Leadership is achieved. We stated that Awakened Leaders are made, not born, fashioned by trial and error. The 21 trial-and-error areas we reviewed in this chapter were:

- Morals and Values
- Ethics
- Integrity, Honesty, and Trust
- Vision
- Respect
- Passion
- Commitment
- Compassion
- Justice
- Kindness
- Forgiveness
- Courage
- Love
- Deep Listening
- Inspired and Inspiring
- Authenticity
- Spiritual Connection
- Multidimensional
- Fulfillment
- Initiative
- Change

These are some points I want to remember from this chapter:
My personal opinions after reading this chapter:

Chapter 4:
The Work Environment of an Awakened Leader

Treat people as if they were what they ought to be and you help them to become what they are capable of being.
Johann Wolfgang Von Goethe

What's Ahead

This chapter reviews the work environment of an Awakened Leader. The chapter specifically focuses on three important aspects of the workplace:

1) Human Resources: How the Awakened Leader perceives this department.
2) Change: Derived from the concept of personal change laid out in Chapter 3, the model of change introduced in this chapter relates to departmental change.
3) Learning: A new all-encompassing strategy toward learning is introduced, based on how Awakened Leaders perceive the place and position of learning in the workplace.

> Awakened Leaders are not limited to certain work environments; you can find them in business corporations, for profit and non-profit organizations, governmental institutions, and in entrepreneurial start-ups. You can even find them in non-leadership positions, for what many of us fail to realize is that we are all leaders of our own lives. We can thus all be Awakened Leaders, regardless of our positions at work.

Besides, some people may have a simple, non-managerial position in one environment, and a very prestigious one in another. They may be the chairperson of a large service organization, or the head of an extended family, or the captain of a sports team, or even the chief of a tribe. The above should also serve as a warning that we should never underestimate people based on the position they have in one environment, because we may encounter them in others at a totally different level.

So Awakened Leaders can be found everywhere. It may be that their mentality is easier to detect in a smaller entity, where people have a closer bond with each other than in a globally operating corporation with hundreds of thousands of employees. But that doesn't mean that the heads of multinational corporations, as well as local presidents and supervisors at different levels, can't be Awakened Leaders. It just depends on one's perception of life. And the more one has learned from life, the more wakeful one becomes.

One point should be stressed as we review work environments: Awakened Leaders are not quitters; by that same token, they also refuse to dwell in toxic environments (see Figure 1.2: The Role of Wakefulness in an Awakened Leader's Life). Depending on their power, they'll try to change the spirit of a negative work environment into a positive one and eradicate the poison of back-stabbing, badmouthing, elbowing, and gossiping. But if they find that this culture is too deeply ingrained into the work environment, and if they find that they can't form a team of allies in this environment to work against the toxic mentality, they will exit, regardless if the job was lusciously paid, and regardless of the organization's place in the stock market. The reason is simple: Awakened Leaders know that toxic environments only do well for a limited time, because they're driven by self-defeating forces such as fear, meanness, and manipulation. So, these environments entail their own future demise. As an Awakened Leader you want no part in an organization that's *unwilling* to strive for the good of all stakeholders: employees, suppliers, customers, shareholders, and the entire community in which the business operates.

So you won't find Awakened Leaders in toxic workplaces: at least, not for long. Either the workplace will become detoxified, or the Awakened Leader will move on (again, see Figure 1.2: The Role of Wakefulness in an Awakened Leader's Life).

You won't find Awakened Leaders in workplaces whose processes are incongruent with the well-being of humanity. Awakened Leaders won't get involved in

- organizations that consistently pollute the environment without finding ways to limit or entirely eradicate their pollution;

- organizations that extract resources from a host environment using unsustainable methods;

- organizations that persistently obstruct learning for their employees;

- organizations that disregard the human factor;

- organizations that show little or no respect for diversity (ages, ethnicities, sexual preferences, religious convictions, physical abilities).

So, what do the environments of Awakened Leaders look like? Let's consider three crucial elements in the organization: human resources, change, and learning.

Human Resources

Awakened Leaders will, above all, maintain close contact with the human resources department of their organizations and make sure this department serves as more than just the hiring and firing division. The Awakened Leader will endorse a new structure for the HR department that will give new meaning to the term HUMAN RESOURCES.

The tasks that this rejuvenated HR unit executes are

Hiring:	Recruiting the right people for the right positions.
Utilizing:	Putting tools and strategies to work that can help improve the workforce.
Managing:	Administering and updating employees' performance reports.
Adapting:	Ensuring mechanisms to upgrade employees' aptitude for change.
Negotiating:	Representing employees' interests in times of change.

Researching: Assisting strategic management in finding ways to upgrade the workforce.

Educating: Facilitating on-the-job or external training for employees when needed.

Suggesting: Reporting to top management regarding employees' training needs.

Organizing: Enhancing inter-organizational activities, as well as family days.

Unifying: Implementing activities to increase employee unity.

Responding: Detecting and responding to signals from workers or worker groups.

Communicating: With top-, mid-, and lower-level management.

Equalizing: Ensuring an optimally performing workforce by implementing diversity.

Synergizing: Creating and sustaining an intra- and extra-organizational team mindset.

Figure 4.1 illustrates how Awakened Leaders can make the HR mission relevant to the organization's needs.

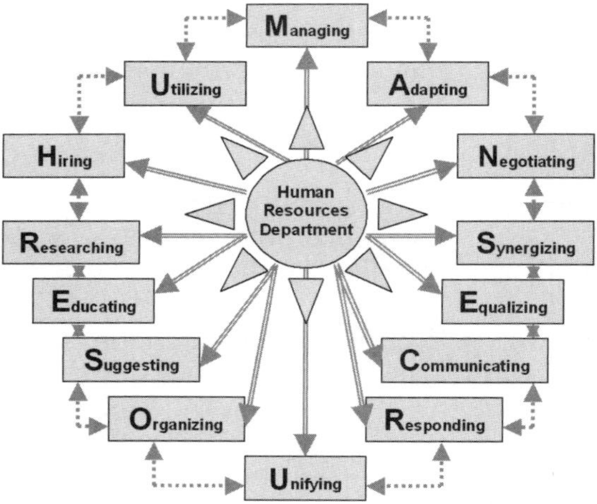

Figure 4.1: **The Awakened Leader's Structure of Human Resources**

Change

If an organization is change-averse, Awakened Leaders avoid getting involved with it because they're highly aware of the speed of change in today's world. Awakened Leaders are therefore also aware of the necessity of promoting the habit of learning among workers at all levels of their organization. They'll do this in order to establish an environment that remains alert toward the usefulness of work processes. Awakened Leaders are particularly aware that it's vital to question the status quo in order to continually upgrade the work itself, thereby ensuring efficiency and return on investment, as well as employees' job satisfaction.

Awakened Leaders therefore constantly emphasize the essence of a change-alert environment by implementing organizational C H A N G E:

Checking: Scanning the work environment to evaluate the relevance of rules and procedures, using an attentive mindset to regularly question the validity of each procedure.

Harvesting: Once a rule or procedure eligible for update or replacement is identified, management should assemble a team of workers who are daily involved with the application of this rule or process. The task of this team is to investigate the rule or process in order to obtain as deep and broad an understanding of its function in the production process, as well as the impact that a change in this rule will have on other inner-departmental and interdepartmental processes. It might be smart to include an *interdepartmental change team* at this stage. In addition to an organization-wide, change-focused team, department workers should form a collaborative team in order to start a brainstorm session regarding possible options.

Advising

Once all viable options are reviewed and listed, the collaborative team will advise top management. This step is particularly important in cases where the most favorable alternative represents a costly investment or a radical change in operations, or if it will have a significant effect on the processes and procedures of other departments. Depending on the size of the change to be implemented, the collaborative team should also request approval to scan the industry and other important stakeholders of the organization (customers, for instance), for other useful alternatives. This may be helpful in determining whether the investment in the considered option would be cost-effective.

Navigating

As soon as top management has approved the industry review, the navigation process can start. This can either be executed by members of the collaborative team, by members of the organization's marketing department, or by external consultants. Regularly navigating the industry is a wise strategy anyway, and should become part of a routine even when there are no rules or processes to be changed. Through regular industry review, the organization can keep itself current in the fast-changing environment and respond to changes quickly. Even better, by regularly navigating the industry, the organization's creative reviewers open the way for innovation that could transform the organization into an industry leader.

Granting

When the navigation process is finalized, the collaborative team will present top management with its overall findings and bring out a recommendation. Top management will then make the decision on the new rule or process to be implemented. Once this is approved, department workers' skills will have to be reviewed in order to ensure that they harbor the right skill set to implement this change. This is where some of the earlier listed HR responsibilities are implemented. Two points are crucial here: 1) There should be *communication* with these workers from a very early stage in order to keep them informed and involved; 2) Depending on the size and complexity of the change, *training* (on-the-job, or through formal education outside the work environment) may be appropriate.

Executing — Once approval from top management and alignment of departmental workers to the new rule or process are achieved, the implementation becomes a fact. It could be wise to conduct close review, particularly in the early stages of the changed process, to limit complications. The process of checking on procedures and rules within the department and throughout the organization should continue even beyond the final stages of execution.

Awakened Leaders should ensure that their organizations are learning-friendly, geared toward transforming change from a *problem* to an *advantage*. They should therefore seek to establish another interdepartmental change team like the one mentioned above, but broader in scope. The members of this team should be cross-functional, derived from various departments and position levels throughout the organization, and all pro-organizational learning and change.

Awakened Leaders should also be aware of another important issue regarding the interdepartmental change team: this team should be altered on a fairly regular base to prevent groupthink, the trend in which people get so used to one another, and obtain such a sense of superiority, that they lose critical perspective in team decisions and become stranded in nonchalance.

Aside from the above, Awakened Leaders should also make sure that two particular types of employees are always present on this team: 1) a representative of higher management, in order to guarantee fast decision-making, and 2) a representative from Human Resources, in order to protect the employees' positions, ensure guidance through the change process, and facilitate employee training when needed. The presence of these two organizational representatives on the team is also crucial in another important regard: they'll ensure constant consideration of the long-term vision of the organization in the options offered for a revision or replacement of a rule or procedure.

Figure 4.2 illustrates an example of how Awakened Leaders can make the continuous process of C H A N G E and organizational learning visible to their co-workers. This figure has much in common with Figure 3.1, which illustrates the C H A N G E cycle of self-reinvention, but in this case the change model is projected on the organizational level rather than on the individual level.

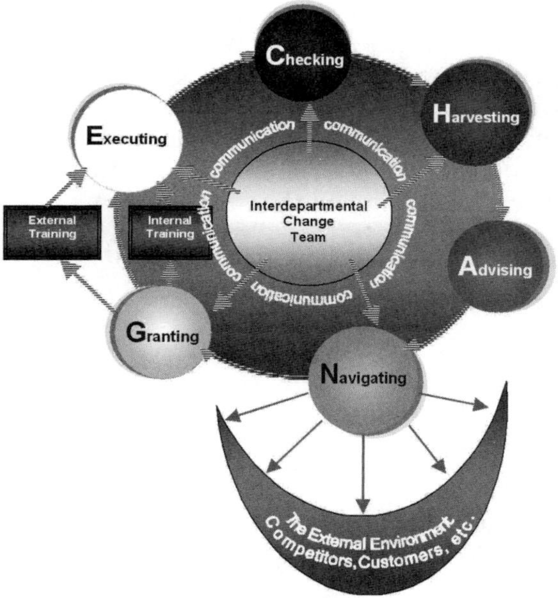

Figure 4.2: **The C H A N G E Cycle of Organizational Reinvention**

Learning

As mentioned above, Awakened Leaders strongly encourage learning within their organization. For that purpose they ensure that learning happens in the most advantageous way to the individuals and to the organization as a whole. The learning method an Awakened Leader should attempt to implement is ***ecumenical learning***, which is an extension to Chris Argyris' double-loop learning. Let's look at this theory.

When Argyris introduced the double-loop learning concept in the 1970s, the theory earned him widespread respect due to the revolutionary insights it presented at that time. Argyris questioned the dominating contemporary perception of single-loop learning, which basically entailed the implementation of set policies and procedures without questioning their foundations or validity in current, oftentimes changed, situations.

In order to explain single-loop learning better, Argyris used a wonderful comparison of this style of learning with a thermostat. The *modus operandi* of a thermostat is that it doesn't question the reasons why it was set on a certain degree, but simply adjusts the temperature when it rises above or falls below that point. So that's what single-loop learning is like: just executing the rules without questioning their efficacy.

In double-loop learning, Argyris stated, there is something more going on: the process of reciprocity was added. To cite from an article this great thinker wrote in 1977 in *Harvard Business Review*: "Double-loop learning is a method that includes the process of detecting and attempting to correct error and the process of questioning underlying organization policies and objectives." So, double-loop learning entails implementing the rules, but *at the same time* questioning whether they still make sense.

Since the introduction of double-loop learning, numerous broadening perspectives and terms have been presented. Terms such as triple-loop learning and multi-loop learning have been used in articles and reports throughout the 90s, and are still in use.

Awakened Leaders, being proponents of optimal advantage for all stakeholders, go one step further than all of the theories mentioned above. They practice organizational learning in a much more comprehensive and revolutionary way: They practice ecumenical learning.

The underlying philosophy of ecumenical learning is a simple one, focused on the massive trend toward globalization. Awakened Leaders realize that you shouldn't only review and question established rules and practices internally—within the current scope of the organization's return on investment and its changed processes and procedures—but also externally, within the scope of the impact of these rules and practices on the organization's performance in its current industry and in industries that it might be targeting for entrance.

After the review process, the impact of the new course of action to be implemented should also be measured against all foreseeable consequences for stakeholders: employees; customers; suppliers; legal, political, economic, and socio-cultural participants; members of the society in which the organization operates; and members of other societies the organization does business with in some way.

In this *impact estimation*, the organization's management, led by an Awakened Leader, won't overlook the effect of this new course of action on the natural environment, which is a growing point of concern to all inhabitants of our planet.

How does such an ecumenical learning process take place in an organization? Here's an example:

1. One of two things happens: A deviation from the routine surfaces, or the insight emerges for a change in the status quo. Note that the ecumenical learning process does not necessarily have to start when a *problem* arises, but that it can become the *logical consequence* of a *continuous quest toward instigating advancement* within all departments of the organization. In order to ensure this movement, Awakened Leaders should consider assembling an interdepartmental team of change activists to hold regular meetings with the various departments in the organization in order to continue sparking enthusiasm toward critical review of established processes and procedures, and, consequently, toward proposed transformation.

2. The department management involved, along with the interdepartmental team of change activists, critically reviews and questions the detected deviation or outmoded process, and its applicability given the current (changed) circumstances for the organization and its environment. At this point, double-loop learning has been implemented with the questioning of rules and procedures to see if they still make sense. It's important here that departmental managers

are updated regularly on the organization's mission and, if possible, on top management's vision for the coming two to five years, in order to evaluate when rules don't just need *questioning*, but *replacement* altogether due to near-future directional changes of the organization. Awakened Leaders should cautiously ensure that this really happens. This updating process could become part of the responsibilities of the interdepartmental team of change activists.

3. Depending on the perceived importance of the process to be adjusted, top management should get involved in order to approve benchmarking (reviewing best practices of similar organizations in the field) and consider alternative options to the rule or procedure. This is necessary to elevate the newly considered solution from a mere incremental innovation to a potentially revolutionary transformation, which will hopefully not only result in enhanced production within the organization, but also in an advancement of the organization's position toward becoming a leader in its industry. Most preferable, of course, would be for the organization to instigate an entire revolution within its industry and other related industries through this new appli-

cation. As an Awakened Leader you'll continuously examine this possibility.

4. While evaluating the potential changes this new application could bring to the organization and its industry, top leadership should also evaluate the ramifications of this application to other stakeholders such as employees, customers, suppliers, societies in which the organization operates and where the organization extracts its resources from, as well as the impact of this change on the natural environment.

5. The learned experiences should regularly be communicated to middle management and subsequent levels to keep all segments of the organization in sync.

Keep in mind that, while ecumenical learning is a powerful process, there are two prerequisites required to make this comprehensive type of learning possible within an organization:

1. Top management must embrace the mindset and subsequently make the call for this comprehensive learning process because of its potential impact and widespread effect within the organization's learning progression. Only within the scope of top management control

can this policy be activated. So if you're an Awakened Leader in top management, that will be easier. However, if your leadership pertains to lower levels of the organization, you'll have to communicate this powerful style of organizational learning to the top first in order to get full cooperation, for only then will ecumenical learning really work.

2. Linked to the above: The organization should be unencumbered by imposing, decelerating hierarchical processes that make communication between departmental management and top-level leadership an unwieldy process.

Awakened Leaders at the head of the organization should ensure that these prerequisites are met.

Figure 4.3 illustrates the flow of information in an ecumenical learning system as described above.

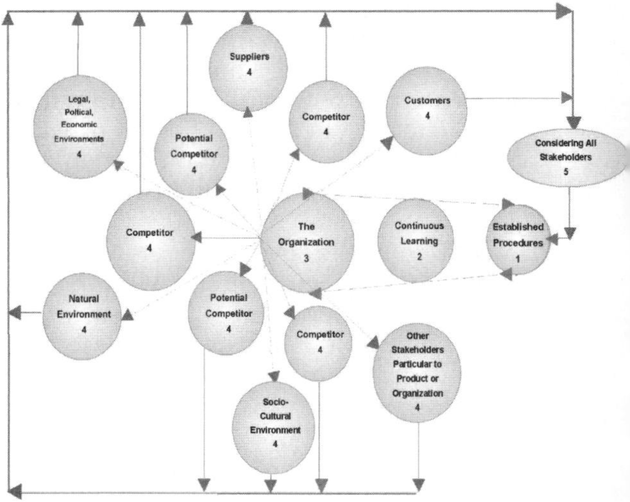

Figure 4.3: Information Flow in Ecumenical Learning Process

exude a pleasant atmosphere. If you're the president or CEO and want to live according to the way of an Awakened Leader, creating such an atmosphere is part of your job description. Co-workers should have no fear of losing a job due to gossiping or backstabbing, because you ensure the workplace is free from such toxic mentalities.

There should, thus, be an atmosphere of mutual respect, understanding, and acceptance in the workplace of an Awakened Leader. There will be open communication, because this type of leader believes in listening to people, in giving each stakeholder a chance of voicing his or her opinion, and in being available. There are no excessive hierarchies in a workplace where an Awakened Leader is in charge.

If possible at all, there will be plants, pictures, paintings and drawings, genuineness, friendliness, and regular events to emphasize that workers are in the first place holistic human beings with families and lives outside of the work environment.

Through all the above-described circumstances you can figure that the employees in a workplace led by an Awakened Leader will be less inhibited than those in workplaces where there's a high level of formality and rigidity.

There will be trust, and there will be encouragement of workers' talents outside of their work-related capacities, because Awakened Leaders know that people have the right to find their way in life, whether that entails staying with the current company or not. And *because* employees know that the Awakened Leader encourages all their efforts, they'll stay with the company; turnover will be extremely low.

In Review

This chapter described the work environment of an Awakened Leader. Employee involvement, communication, and diversity embracement were among the elements emphasized. The chapter discussed some of the environments that Awakened Leaders will avoid. It subsequently reviewed three crucial elements in the workplace of an Awakened Leader: Human Resources, change, and ecumenical learning, each illustrated with a model for clarification.

Sources cited in Chapter 4:

- Argyris, C. (1977). Double loop learning in organizations. *Harvard Business Review, 55*(5), 115.
- Baas, L. (2005). *Cleaner production and industrial ecology; dynamic aspects of the introduction and dissemination of new concepts in industrial practice.* Delft: Eburon Academic Publishers.
- Flood, R. L., & Romm, N. R. A. (1996). *Diversity management: Triple loop learning.* West Sussex: Wiley.
- Flood, R. L., & Romm., N. R. A. (1996). Contours of diversity management and triple loop learning. *Kybernetes, 25*(7/8), 154-164.
- Hargrove, R. (1996). Masterful coaching. *Executive Excellence, 13*(7), 18-19.
- Isaacs, W. N. (1993). Taking flight: Dialogue, collective thinking, and organizational learning. *Organizational Dynamics, 22*(2), 24-39.
- Li, Y., Bontcheva, K., Aswani, N., Peters, W., & Cunningham, H. (2005, 31 Dec.). *D2.5.2 report: Quantitative evaluation tools and corpora: version 2.* University of Sheffield. Retrieved on March 9, 2006, from http://www.sekt-project.org/rd/deliverables/wp02/sekt-d-2-5-2-Quantitive%20Evaluation%20Tools%20and%20Corpora.pdf
- Pruijt, H. D. (1996). *The fight against Taylorism in Europe: Strategies, achievements in job design and technology, setbacks, obstacles, chances for upgrading work.* Erasmus University, Rotterdam.
- Taket, A. (1998). Diversity management: Triple loop learning. *The Journal of the Operational Research Society, 49*(3), 293-296.

These are some points I want to remember from this chapter:
My personal opinions after reading this chapter:

Chapter 5: What an Awakened Leader Will Do

An army of sheep led by a lion would defeat an army of lions led by a sheep.
Arab Proverb

What's Ahead

In this chapter we'll make a subtle shift in perspective: We'll move from the internal qualities of Awakened Leaders to the behavior this type of leader displays toward employees, shareholders, customers, suppliers, members of the community, and others.

While this chapter, like those preceding it, is by no means exhaustive, it should get you thinking about the behavior of Awakened Leaders toward others.

Enlightened Activity

"I do what I say, I say what I think, and I think what I feel." –Gandhi

This statement captures in the simplest way the concept of enlightened activity. It involves unity and purity of our thoughts, and congruence between our thoughts and our actions. Wakeful people engage in this behavior because it is simpler to be straightforward than to keep track of various codes of conduct. Employees don't need much time to distinguish a genuine leader from an overly complex one. The behavior of Awakened Leaders may very well be the only area in which homogeneity is efficacious: Awakened Leaders walk their talk.

Peace

"Every kind of peaceful cooperation among men is primarily based on mutual trust and only secondarily on institutions such as courts of justice and police." –Albert Einstein

Awakened Leaders exhibit a heightened level of trust, compassion, kindness, and goodness, in order to establish peace in their environment. They start out every relationship with trust, and their instinct to always see the positive *first* makes them buoyant and resilient. Yet, their behavior isn't impulsive. They're wise enough to remain wakeful, but they prevent negative thoughts and feelings as much as possible. They refrain from violent behavior in any sense, even in the subtler forms. Therefore, you won't see them engage in crass office politics, using harsh words, or insulting or exploiting people.

Vision

"*Only he who can see the invisible can do the impossible.*" –Frank Gaines

Awakened Leaders develop their vision from past successes, but even more from past failures. The lessons learned from these failures sharpened the leaders' ability to recognize opportunities. Awakened Leaders therefore have a vision for the organization as well as for themselves. The organizational vision will be one that involves the well-being of all stakeholders in the long term. The Awakened Leader articulates the vision well, allowing all stakeholders to identify and realize the meaning and purpose of their activities.

Collaboration

"The moment we break faith with one another, the sea engulfs us and the light goes out." –James Baldwin

Awakened Leaders are aware of the power of collaboration, acceptance, and mutual respect. Moreover, they're aware of the abundance of knowledge present in a diverse workforce. A diverse workforce harbors many cultures and mindsets, and therefore, perspectives that everyone can learn from. Awakened Leaders will therefore support the diversity mindset, and encourage acceptance and teamwork in order to achieve greater heights for the organization as well as all workers individually.

Morality

"The moral virtues, then, are produced in us neither by nature nor against nature. Nature, indeed, prepares in us the ground for their reception, but their complete formation is the product of habit." –Aristotle

If Aristotle is right, we should practice caution after the storm of immoral practices from Enron, Tyco, Martha Stewart, Omnimedia, and others in recent years. We don't want these behavioral patterns to become habit, and therefore, a moral standard. This realization drives Awakened Leaders toward telling the truth even when it is unpleasant or embarrassing, working diligently to build trust within the organization and encouraging others to practice integrity as well.

Communication

"*There are four ways, and only four ways, in which we have contact with the world. We are evaluated and classified by these four contacts: what we do, how we look, what we say, and how we say it.*" –Dale Carnegie

Awakened Leaders communicate with passion and compassion. They voice their perspectives clearly, but they listen even better. Through their two main behavioral pillars, authenticity and emotional intelligence (see Chapter 1), they communicate on various levels. They pay attention to the spoken and the unspoken word. They show genuine interest for their co-workers beyond the boundaries of the workplace. And, as mentioned above, they walk their talk.

Generosity

"*What I gave I have, what I spent I had; and what I left I lost.*" *–Robert of Doncaste*

Generosity entails giving, and giving entails receiving, just as Robert of Doncaste asserted. Awakened Leaders are generous toward their workers and the community. Their generosity isn't limited to financial donations, but entails praise and rewards as well. Awakened Leaders enjoy making people feel good about themselves, helping them grow, and sharing the rewards when the organization is successful. They know how good it feels to do well. They cherish the sparkle of gratitude they receive when they're generous, and use this sparkle as an encouragement to be even more giving in the future.

Motivation Toward Growth

"*A message prepared in the mind reaches a mind; a message prepared in a life reaches a life.*" –Bill Gothard

Although Awakened Leaders readily offer a pep talk or a shoulder when needed, the greatest source of motivation they have to offer their workers is an exemplary life. Knowing that the Awakened Leader has had his or her share of ups and downs encourages employees to demonstrate resilience as well. Knowing that the leader is genuine encourages workers to be genuine too. Knowing that the leader works hard encourages them to work hard as well.

Decrease Turnover

"The greater the loyalty of a group toward the group, the greater is the motivation among the members to achieve the goals of the group, and the greater the probability that the group will achieve its goals." –Rensis Likert

Awakened Leaders nurture a team spirit in their workplaces, but they also acknowledge individual workers' qualities. They therefore encourage each worker to be the best person he or she can be, even if it means the person could someday leave the organization in pursuit of that goal. The Awakened Leader doesn't fear this, because he or she knows that workers who feel valued and encouraged won't leave very easily, even when offered prestigious positions elsewhere.

Spiritual Practice and Dignity

"The foundations of a person are not in matter but in spirit." –Ralph Waldo Emerson

Awakened Leaders believe that every person is more than just a body. Through their deep self-connection, they're able to connect deeply with others as well. They value relationships and the welfare of human beings.

If they face a tough business decision, such as a lay off, they'll communicate this in a manner respectful of workers, families, and futures. An apt example is Ouimet-Tomasso Inc., a food processing plant in Montreal that provides the traditional support systems to people who are laid off. Yet in addition, each manager meets one-on-one, face-to-face on two separate occasions with any employee who has been laid off. There's no agenda; the purpose of the meeting is to acknowledge and respect the difficulty of the transition the former employees will undergo as a result of the loss of their position. That's an example of Awakened Leadership through spiritual practice and dignity.

Humane and Ethical

"The character ethic, which I believe to be the foundation of success, teaches that there are basic principles of effective living, and that people can only experience true success and enduring happiness as they learn and integrate these principles into their basic character." –Stephen R. Covey

Awakened Leaders are committed to bring forth products and services that benefit humanity and don't cause deliberate harm. As an extension of that commitment, they demand the highest ethical standards in business, even if it means sacrificing some profits, only because they hold themselves to the same standards.

Change-Driven

"The first step toward change is awareness. The second step is acceptance." –Nathaniel Branden

Awakened Leaders regularly cast a critical eye on the status quo, as we discussed in chapters 3 and 4 in the context of change. However, it isn't only organizational processes and procedures that these leaders regularly question; they also review the mission and core values of the organization on an ongoing basis.

Leading by Example

"*The first great gift we can bestow on others is a good example.*" –Thomas Morell

Awakened Leaders lead by example, by what they do everyday. And because they're aware of that, they'll be consistent, genuine, and balanced. They'll also demonstrate that they have their priorities in order. They'll be organized enough to prevent issues from becoming problems, thus they'll take on tasks that are important *before* they become pressing matters.

Getting the Right People on Board

"*What we need to do is learn to work in the system, by which I mean that everybody, every team, every platform, every division, every component is there not for individual competitive profit or recognition, but for contribution to the system as a whole on a win-win basis.*" –W. Edwards Deming

Awakened Leaders make every effort to find the right people for the organization. In his book *Good to Great*, Jim Collins compares great organizations with buses filled with people who are enjoying the ride rather than worrying about the destination. As an Awakened Leader you want to make sure you have those types of people on board—people who love being there because they trust you as the driver of the bus, and they love the other passengers (colleagues, customers, suppliers). There's a family atmosphere, so even if you come to believe that the bus needs to change direction, you'll be able to communicate that to your passengers without getting thrown off the bus.

Goal-Oriented Through Shared Governance

"*The reason most people never reach their goals is that they don't define them, or ever seriously consider them as believable or achievable. Winners can tell you where they are going, what they plan to do along the way, and who will be sharing the adventure with them.*" –Denis Watley

Awakened Leaders know that goals are met much faster and with much more gratification for all if everyone is involved. These leaders therefore establish a system of shared governance in their organization to build consensus.

Big goals are more readily attained when they're made up of smaller, intermediate goals that allow for celebrations to keep the spirits up. There are clear lines of responsibility, and everyone has a part to play.

Improvement-Focused

"You cannot hope to build a better world without improving the individuals. To that end each of us must work for his own improvement, and at the same time share a general responsibility for all humanity, our particular duty being to aid those to whom we think we can be most useful." –Marie Curie

Awakened Leaders approach issues from the perspective of, "What can we do better?" rather than "What did we do wrong?" These leaders ask, "Where and how can we go to the next level?" and will make sure that co-workers get involved in the decision-making process, for that's how shared governance works.

Trust-Building

"Trust is the lubrication that makes it possible for organizations to work." –Warren Bennis

Awakened Leaders realize that it may take time for workers to buy into their vision for the organization. In that case communication and openness are the best methods of building trust until co-workers start seeing the sense of the vision and get on board. Awakened Leaders know that in these cases their behavior is of the highest essence. An attitude of cohesion creates a shared sense of ownership, not just of ideas, but of the group's concerted effort.

Unity of Happiness and Success

"*Success is not the key to happiness. Happiness is the key to success. If you love what you are doing, you will be successful.*" –Albert Schweitzer

Awakened Leaders consider happiness and success interchangeable. They're not likely to measure success by their level of income or the value of their belongings. For them, success goes hand in hand with a general feeling of contentment and being where and what they want to be.

Life experiences and readings have shown Awakened Leaders that many people who gain status seek treatment for depression because they're so lonely, and there are many people unable to trust anyone around them for fear of not really being liked for who they are, but accepted for their financial wealth or high position. Awakened Leaders also understand how many people have taken their own lives, leaving behind millions of dollars, because they realized that *having it all* did not necessarily mean *having all that matters*.

Awakened Leaders are conscientious analysts who observe how and why wealthy business people have gained their success. And, like many others, Awakened Leaders came to the conclusion that the majority of tycoons are successful because they do what they like best: Microsoft's Bill Gates, Apple's Steve Jobs, and Dell's Michael Dell all started out as computer lovers, and they still are; Virgin's Richard Branson started as an entrepreneur, and he still is, even though he no longer needs to do it for the money; GE's remarkable former CEO Jack Welch, although an engineer by education, found his passion in leading people, and continued doing that until his retirement; Oprah Winfrey loved being a talk show host, and continues to do that in spite of her multiple billions today. Whether these people are truly happy or not we may never really know, but we do know that they have a few things in common: 1) They're financially wealthy; 2) They say that they really like what they do, which makes them stick to it and do it well. They seem to be content with where and who they are.

Which brings me to another interesting, related topic—ambition as a vehicle toward bringing happiness and success together. In a Forbes.com survey conducted April 2005 (at the time of my review 35,713 people had already voted) the following reasons were given as possible sources behind the wealth of the super-rich people in the world: ambition: 32%; connections, ingenuity, and inheritance: 13% each; greed: 9%; intelligence: 5%; arrogance: 4%; generosity: 1%; "Don't know": 6%; none of the above: 4%.

There's something to say for ambition being by far the leader on this list, demonstrating that, when you have a drive toward achieving something, you also have a much larger chance of reaching your goal. As a former teacher of mine used to say, "If you do what you like most, you will do it well and consistently; you will be happy, and the rewards will automatically come, even if rewards are not your priority." Or as Confucius said, "Find something you love to do, and you will never work a day in your life."

Maybe that's the secret of the super rich: the majority of them do what they like most and therefore invest more of themselves in it than others are willing to. Unfortunately, society has a tendency to measure success superficially by material wealth gained, often overlooking the gratifying part. But many affluent people are probably happy with who and what they are *regardless* of the magnitude of their bank account. That has to be our ultimate reason for considering them successful. Those who are low-spirited despite their billions are just financially well-off; if they're not happy, they're not successful in the essential sense of the word.

And then there are those who don't want the affluence—they just want to have enough to pay the bills and live a simple, uncomplicated life. No big deal for those souls—just undemanding days of family life or devotion to the things they consider fun. Even though those people's names may never reach the newspapers, no one can say that they're less successful than Gates, Jobs, Dell, Branson, Welch, or Winfrey.

Ever considered that the ambition of unknown yet contented individuals may just be to *remain* a simple soul, and that it should therefore not be considered any less of an ambition?

In conclusion: Affluence is only enjoyable when one is also content, yet, contentment has nothing to do with being affluent. Contented people are happy, with or without much money. Contented people are successful; therefore, happy people are successful.

Awakened Leaders know that, and they walk the talk.

In Review

This chapter presented specific behaviors of Awakened Leaders toward all those they interact with. The patterns discussed were:

- Enlightened Activity
- Peace
- Vision
- Collaboration
- Morality
- Communication
- Generosity
- Motivation Toward Growth
- Decrease Turnover
- Spiritual Practice and Dignity
- Humanity and Ethics
- Change Orientation
- Leading by Example
- Getting the Right People on Board
- Goal Orientation Through Shared Governance
- Improvement Focus
- Trust-Building
- Unity of Happiness and Success

These are some points I want to remember from this chapter:

My personal opinions after reading this chapter:

Chapter 6:

What an Awakened Leader Won't Do

To lead people, walk beside them. . . .
As for the best leaders, the people do not notice their existence. The next best, the people honor and praise. The next, the people fear; and the next, the people hate. When the best leader's work is done the people say, "We did it ourselves."
Lao Tzu

What's Ahead

This chapter will be the exact opposite of the previous. We'll now review behavior that Awakened Leaders refrain from in their approach toward employees, shareholders, customers, suppliers, members of the community, and others.

Again, this chapter, like those preceding it, is by no means exhaustive. But it should get you thinking about the behaviors you may want to unlearn if you'd like to become an Awakened Leader.

Advancing at Others' Expense

"Do no harm to the earth,
she is your mother.
Being is more important than having.
Never promote yourself
at another's expense.
Hold life sacred; treat it with reverence.
Allow each person
the dignity of his or her labor."

–[DGH3]Arthur Dobrin

Awakened Leaders won't deliberately hurt others to advance their own career or organizational goals. Awakened Leaders have an advantage in that, through their wakefulness, they're also creative. They've seen enough of the world to know the broad variety of possibilities, and they'd rather engage in peaceful, creative methods to establish their advancement than negative, hurtful, unrewarding practices. Because Awakened Leaders believe that good instigates good and bad instigates bad, they seek to do well by doing good.

Bending the Law

"*Laws are not masters, but servants, and he rules them, who obeys them.*" –Ward Becker

Awakened Leaders won't bend the law for organizational or personal benefit. They don't believe in situational ethics. In other words, Awakened Leaders exhibit the same values regardless of the situation or circumstance.

Engaging in Fake Behavior

"*The great enemy of clear language is insincerity. When there's a gap between one's real and one's declared aims, one turns as it were instinctively to long words and exhausted idioms, like a cuttlefish spurting out ink.*" –George Orwell

Awakened Leaders don't engage in phony behavior in order to get ahead. They're too straightforward and genuine for that, and they believe in the Golden Rule: treat others as you want to be treated.

Being Unethical and Immoral

"I know only that what is moral is what you feel good after and what is immoral is what you feel bad after." –Ernest Hemingway

Awakened Leaders won't engage in unethical or immoral behavior. They're too much in contact with their inner source and know too well the internal punishment that waits when their conscience is disturbed.

Being Alienated

"The alienated person is as out of touch with himself as he is out of touch with any other person. He, like the others, is experienced as things are experienced: with the senses and with common sense, but at the same time, without being positively related to oneself and to the world outside." –Erich Fromm

Awakened Leaders will avoid neither people nor issues that need attention. Awakened Leaders are relationship-oriented; they realize that every issue should be handled in the shortest possible time and to the advantage of all.

Being Autocratic

"Companies used to be able to function with autocratic bosses. We don't live in that world anymore." –Rosabeth Moss Kanter

Awakened Leaders are leaders in today's flexible, interconnected, awakened world. They therefore refrain from being autocratic, not just because autocracy is an outdated mode, but even more because autocratic behavior is against their nature. Awakened Leaders are not demanding, coercive, mean, stingy, or greedy, nor do they damage the lives of those they serve.

Being Disrespectful

"Throughout life people will make you mad, disrespect you, and treat you bad. Let God deal with the things they do, 'cause hate in your heart will consume you too." –Will Smith

Awakened Leaders don't show disrespect to other people. They treat all employees equally, regardless of their position in the workplace. They don't micromanage, but they enable workers to make their own decisions as often as possible. They are not reluctant to delegate, and never say anything negative about one employee in front of another. And if they get disrespected, they think of the quote above and move on.

Manipulating Others

"I do not deny that many appear to have succeeded in a material way by cutting corners and by manipulating associates, both in their professional and in their personal lives. But material success is possible in this world and far more satisfying when it comes without exploiting others." –Alan Greenspan

Awakened Leaders don't hold people accountable outside of their realm of responsibility. However, they do evaluate performance, because that's part of their job, part of helping the organization grow. Awakened Leaders know that sometimes corrections are necessary, and they're aware when there's a need for intervention.

However, they don't set employees up against one another. They refrain from creating in-groups and out-groups. They just don't allow that to happen because they know such a Machiavellian concept won't lead the organization toward longitudinal prosperity.

Manipulation only works for a short time, and afterward you may find yourself in even bigger trouble than before. Some leaders manipulate all the time to distract people from real problems. One leader who was struggling with a number of interpersonal issues changed the parking system on his staff overnight as a distraction tactic. He stated, “We no longer have assigned parking places here,” and staff members were outraged. They were so upset that they became entirely absorbed by this new rule. This leader had managed to manipulate his workers, and for a while it worked. The staff members didn’t focus on all the other problems that were going on. But the question remains whether this strategy worked in the long run.

Another leader in an academic environment did something similar. Student revolutions were disrupting the peace on campus, and there were marches and rally protests everywhere. So this president ordered the food caterer to serve the worst food possible that day. The students got distracted and started arguing about the food, thus dividing forces. Indeed, manipulation may work for a while, but Awakened Leaders avoid negotiating long-term solutions through short-term peevishness.

Doing Harm Toward Any Form of Existence

"If I knew something that would serve my country but would harm mankind, I would never reveal it; for I am a citizen of humanity first and by necessity, and a citizen of France second, and only by accident." –Charles de Montesquieu

Awakened Leaders don't do deliberate harm to any living being, because they have a sense of connection with all of existence. Their respect for life stretches beyond humanity. They don't kill, hurt, or capture for their own pleasure, due to the high level of compassion they harbor and the deep thinking they have done about life. Awakened Leaders know that human beings are not more or less than any other form of life. Derived from this conviction, they respect humans, plants, animals, and everything that results from these forms of life.

Being Judgmental

"*We should be lenient in our judgment, because often the mistakes of others would have been ours had we had the opportunity to make them.*" –R. L. Dr. Alsaker

Awakened Leaders are cautious about falling prey to judgmental behavior. They know how easy it is to stereotype; consequently, they judge people who have good intentions on the basis of the behavior of other members of their age, ethnic, gender, or skills group. Awakened Leaders will therefore not be harsh in criticism, but engage in more creative ways to guide others toward the right action. They're not hasty in decision-making. They're not unkind, and they refrain from any action that could be interpreted negatively.

Getting Priorities Out of Order

"*Keep in mind that you are always saying 'no' to something. If it isn't to the apparent, urgent things in your life, it is probably to the most fundamental, highly important things. Even when the urgent is good, the good can keep you from your best, keep you from your unique contribution, if you let it.*" –Stephen R. Covey

Awakened Leaders are aware of the strain that striving for achievements can cause. They understand the toll that the realization of dreams can take. They've taken note of the priority mistakes some of the world's most admired leaders have made:

- Mother Teresa left home at age 18, never to see her mother again.

- Jesus Christ demonstrated little closeness to his family and failed to encourage family ties for his disciples as well.

- Gandhi belittled his wife and held his sons to unreasonable standards of conduct. His grandson, Arun Gandhi, writes, "In no way was Gandhi kind to Ba (his wife) in the first 20 to 30 years of marriage. He gave the orders and she obeyed." Arun continues, "While Mohandas (the Mahatma) experimented with truth, Kasturba experienced it."

- M. L. King Jr. was known as a first-rate adulterer. Authors repeatedly commented on King's voracious extramarital sexual appetite, and described him as a charismatic personality who attracted many women to his hotel rooms.

- Fidel Castro divorced his wife and abandoned his firstborn even before he became Cuba's leader. This leader conceived children with various women throughout his life, but failed to maintained intimate contact with the majority of his offspring.

- Nelson Mandela, married three times, was an inadequate parent to his children. A 1994 article published in *The Economist* stated the following: "Even as a free man, [Mandela] was a rotten husband to both his wives. At their wedding, Winnie's father had warned her that she was marrying a man who was already married to the struggle."

One may question whether these great leaders really needed to abandon their loved ones in order to fulfill their important calling. It seems quite possible to fulfill a dream without abandoning other parts of one's life.

Awakened Leaders learn from the mistakes their predecessors made in life, and try to keep their priorities in order. They try to maintain a *balance* between realizing their dreams and embracing their loved ones.

In Review

This chapter presented behavior that Awakened Leaders try to avoid. The behavioral patterns discussed were:

- Advancing at Others' Expense
- Bending the Law
- Engaging in Fake Behavior
- Being Unethical and Immoral
- Being Alienated
- Being Autocratic
- Being Disrespectful
- Doing Harm Toward Any Form of Existence
- Being Judgmental
- Getting Priorities Out of Order

These are some points I want to remember from this chapter:

My personal opinions after reading this chapter:

Chapter 7:
The Easy Part of Being an Awakened Leader

To lead the people, walk behind them.
Lao Tzu

What's Ahead

In this chapter we'll look into the things that come easily to those who practice Awakened Leadership. The chapter reviews behavior that makes leading in any environment easy for this type of leader. We'll find that the common factor in all these characteristics is their foundation in human decency, respect, and acceptance.

One Hat

The most obvious and important advantage of Awakened Leadership is that you don't have to remember to put on different hats for different circumstances because you are always yourself: always genuine, always authentic. If you know your inner self and are aware of your own wakefulness, you don't have to check your soul at the door anymore. If you tell the truth, you don't have to remember falsehoods. You're spared from the complexity of juggling many attitudinal balls in the air, because there will only be one ball in the air for you. You're the same person at home, at work, in school, or in church. You realized long ago that it's a lot of work to maintain different personalities toward different audiences. To an Awakened Leader, life is very easy in this regard. And if you look at it this way, only the awakened ones among us live in awareness of the moment. The rest of us are constantly doing mathematics, calculating whom to impress and how.

Real Freedom

Although this issue is related to the previous topic, it contains some important points to ponder. Awakened people live with a sense of *attachment*—a sense of oneness with the world—yet also with a healthy sense of *detachment* where necessary. If you can live with detachment, you're a free person. Awakened people know that true freedom does not lie in pre-defined boundaries, but in obtaining a state of liberty in your mind. Through this state, you learn to become a person of no rank regardless of your assigned position. Being a person of no rank means that you don't specifically belong to anything. You just are what you are. You live your life without any psychological complication. And that's the easy part of being an Awakened Leader. It may not be as easy for all people, because society has taught us to be specific in determining the groups we want to belong to and then stick with them. Yet practice and critical thinking can cause miracles.

Yielding

Another thing that's easy for an Awakened Leader is yielding. It's like giving another driver the right of way when you don't have to. The consequence is that you become happy for yielding; the other person is pleasantly surprised by encountering such an unexpected favor, and the road is a lot safer. It works the same way in workplaces.

Yielding to others on various occasions sets a pleasant atmosphere and creates mutuality. That's the awakened way of being. And the benefit is that you make yourself and everyone else happy by being what you are without complications.

Values

Yet another easy aspect about being an Awakened Leader is that you don't have to figure out what to do in difficult situations because you've already committed yourself to a set of values and principles that guide your actions. You know your personal taboos and how to respond to them, so decision-making becomes a whole lot easier.

Focus

Because you've decided to live by your own value system (in- and outside the workplace), your whole life becomes much easier, because the stress is gone. You realize how easy it is to examine and understand where you're going, which brings a lot of vitality and passion to your life and work, rather than being anemic and non-committed to where you stand.

Vision

Following your calling, thus realizing your dreams, is another easy thing about being an Awakened Leader. Because you don't allow yourself to be driven by money or prestige, but mainly by what you consider worthwhile and good, you can focus on your dreams without worrying. You've probably already figured out that if you do what you like, the rewards will automatically follow. And because you're not money-driven, but rather value-driven, it's easier to follow your dreams.

Connectedness

This point touches somewhat deeper: When you're an Awakened Leader, you never perceive yourself as being alone. You consider yourself supported by a power that's much greater and wiser than you. You're connected. You have a sense of oneness with everything. Through listening you receive guidance and direction. Mostly, the answers come from within. That's why Awakened Leaders should always allot time for contemplating, meditating, praying, or communicating with those whom they trust. If you live up to your awakened values and are caring toward co-workers, you'll find that oftentimes they won't need to be controlled or managed. Instead, you'll help them unleash *their* passion and creativity as well, creating a sense of fulfillment in all.

Human Decency

An important factor that will be easy for you as an Awakened Leader is being a decent person. This means that you'll never choose to gain the world if it entails losing your soul. However, it doesn't mean that you're against making profits or establishing organizational growth. Not at all! You still focus on these issues, but in a less apprehensive way. And *because* of that everything becomes more rewarding. Thus, being an Awakened Leader is helpful to you, and as a result of that, to others as well.

Improvement Orientation

Another easy aspect of being an Awakened Leader is that all your actions are geared toward improvement. Not just improvement for yourself, but for all stakeholders: workers, customers, the community, the environment as a whole, *and* yourself. So, as an Awakened Leader, you enhance the lives of others by encouraging them to improve themselves.

Wakefulness

It's easy to be an Awakened Leader once you've defined your own wakefulness, because then you know exactly who you are, what you are, and where you are going. You can't easily be taken off track. If you have yet to define your own wakefulness, you can begin by distilling your various perspectives down to one cohesive, principled viewpoint.

Sensitivity

Sensitivity comes easy to you as an Awakened Leader. However, sensitivity can also be a difficult matter. The point is, you have to be careful about becoming overly sensitive. There are two sides to everything, and you have to be cautious not to fall prey to over-embellishment. Having a balanced degree of sensitivity will enable you to see the whole picture as well as the details. While you enjoy this dual-perception capability, however, be aware in your communications with your co-workers that they might not see the details relating to the whole in the same way as you. Being sensitive to diverse points of view will help you find commonality before confusion can germinate.

Naturalness and Temperance

It's easy if you can keep calm when others don't. When you maintain a genuine foundation, it becomes easier to respect and understand others' viewpoints. And then it also becomes easy to get out of the way and let situations dissolve when they need to. Sometimes issues just handle themselves, and if you can recognize when that's the case and let things transpire without constant force, that's always easier.

In Review

In this chapter we reviewed a number of behavioral traits that come easy to Awakened Leaders. The easy conducts reviewed in this chapter were:

- One Hat
- Real Freedom
- Yielding
- Values
- Focus
- Vision
- Connectedness
- Human Decency
- Improvement Orientation
- Wakefulness
- Sensitivity
- Naturalness and Temperance

At the end of Chapter 8 you'll find a figure that provides an overview of the easy and the hard things in the performance of Awakened Leadership.

These are some points I want to remember from this chapter:
My personal opinions after reading this chapter:

Chapter 8:

The Hard Part of Being an Awakened Leader

If you have no character to lose,
people will have no faith in you.
Mahatma Gandhi

What's Ahead

In this chapter we'll review the difficult aspects of the practice of Awakened Leadership. The chapter will begin with a discussion of common corporate behavior that can make leading difficult for this type of leader. As we'll see, the common factor in all of these difficulties is the pressure that society and its members have placed upon themselves to conform to misaligned, misguided standards of conduct.

Pressure and Politics

It's hard to deal with the constant pressure of today's hectic corporate environment, to compromise ethics and values for short-term results, career advancement, and political advantage. It's hard to withstand the pressure of fitting with elements of your organizational culture that may not be consistent with your values.

Uncooperativeness and Standards

It's also hard to follow your calling and dream in a world that may be less than supportive. What I mean here is that our civilization has created certain rules and perspectives that we've learned to obey. It may be the pressure of having to follow in the footsteps of previous generations. If your father was a medical doctor, the whole family may expect you to become one too, even if you dream of doing something else. And then there's the pressure of living up to standards: the clothes you wear, the car you drive, the house you live in, and the neighborhood you reside in. They may not be opportune given your dreams, but the pressure may be too heavy to withstand. If you want to pursue a goal that your company's shareholders don't believe in, or that requires an entire turnaround of the company's focus, it may be hard to realize *that dream* regardless if it feels good to you. If the pressure of the bystanders in your circle is significant, it may be hard to pursue your acts as an Awakened Leader, at least early in your life. As you mature, things may become different, and you may decide that you'll pursue your dreams anyway regardless of what others think.

Ego Management

It can be hard to manage your ego. Most people become leaders *because* of an immense ego. And there are some who say that nothing meaningful gets done in the world without a whole lot of ego. But it can come back to bite you. As you become more successful, you tend to think that it is due to your competencies, your wisdom, and your experience. If you put too much weight on this idea, you may forget that it was also your followers' competencies, wisdom, and experiences that helped create organizational success. You may stop listening. You may begin believing that you know all the answers, and you can cut yourself off from your own wakeful guidance when this happens. Humility is important for an Awakened Leader, and this is sometimes hard when you're financially highly successful.

Remaining Authentic

Another thing that can be difficult is managing the fine line between deeply living your own values and creating an environment that nurtures the individual paths of other organization members. There may be a clash in authenticities (genuine people who just don't get along), and therefore a need for a decision on who should exit and who should stay. In these cases you may find yourself placed before a dilemma of having to release valuable individuals for the long-term welfare of the organization, or—if you're not on the highest branch of the organizational tree—you may receive your own invitation to exit.

Inner-Connection

If you're not tuned in to who you really are—you're still searching and still in limbo regarding some crucial standpoints you should take—it can be very difficult to be an Awakened Leader. Not that there's anything wrong with that. We're all subject to change, and our insights and beliefs may alter at times. If the process of shaping your soul is ongoing, you may find it hard to be an

Awakened Leader because you're still in the process of awakening.

Incompatibility

Another problem may occur when you're situated in a major corporate entity where your style of leadership is neither promoted nor a part of the corporate culture. In that case it's difficult for you as a person to step up and be an Awakened Leader, because your way is simply not understood, and the support and reward mechanisms are not in place for it.

Consistency

You need a level of consistency to be an Awakened Leader. It's what your followers expect of you, and that may be difficult. There's always the generic temptation to deviate from your wakefulness, but essential material and positional rewards will be more attractive for those who are corrupt, money-driven, or uncaring about the impact of their decisions for stakeholders than for those who are conscious, ethical, and fair.

Accountability

It may sometimes be hard to be an Awakened Leader because you're held accountable to yourself and to others. You're the one responsible for where everybody's going. There may be set core values and mission statements, but if you, as the Awakened Leader, don't make sure they're truly lived within the institution, people will hold you accountable and either think or say: "You're not doing what you said."

Material Rewards

Another difficult thing could the perception that being an Awakened Leader doesn't pay. People want to be rewarded materialistically; they want to see dollars, so they think that wakefulness, with its beautiful traits such as emotional intelligence and authenticity, honesty, respect, acceptance, and understanding is something to be practiced on Sundays or in word but not deed. The difficult part for people to see is that being awakened is a call that each of us should listen to on our human journey. The Swiss-born philosopher and traditionalist Fritjof Schuon asserts that if metaphysics could be taught to everyone, there wouldn't be any non-believers, for if people are able to see the underlying unity behind diversity, and if they're able to see that their welfares are interconnected, no one will endanger another's welfare. So, being able to see the underlying advantage for all is wakefulness. But because many people don't see that, they end up engaging in various other practices that have their own ripple effect. The inability of many of us to see that the spiritual basis of life is win-win for all makes it hard to be an Awakened Leader.

Yielding

Yielding was listed as an easy element in Awakened Leadership, yet it surfaces here as a difficult one as well, for yielding may be particularly hard in an aggressive corporate setting. It seems that many of us don't understand what Christ meant when he said "the last will be the first"—the corporate world surely doesn't. Yet, if you understand the advantage of being last, you'll find two miracles happening: 1) you'll have time to grow internally; and 2) you'll be able to serve. And those who serve are leaders. Yet, for many people that's still hard to see, which can make yielding difficult.

Socrates once pointed out that if people were able to *see* what was wrong, they wouldn't do it. And if they still did it, then there would be no reform possible and nothing could be done. On a lighter note, here's a funny way of explaining one of the advantages that yielding can bring about. It's based on an old joke: A sales rep, an administration clerk, and their Awakened Leader are walking together on their way to lunch when they find an antique oil lamp. They pick it up, rub it, and a genie comes out. The genie says: "I'll grant each of you one wish." "Me first! Me first!" exclaims the administrative clerk. "I want to be in the Bahamas driving a speedboat without a care in the world." Poof! She's gone. "Me next! Me next!" says the sales rep. "I want to be in Hawaii, relaxing on the beach with my personal masseuse, an endless supply of Piña Coladas, and the love of my life." Poof! He's gone. "O.K., you're up," says the genie to the Awakened Leader. The leader simply says, "I'm glad they're having fun, but please have them back at work safe and sound after lunch." Interesting illustration of the advantage of yielding, isn't it?

Preferences

Because being a leader is a very ego-driven position, it's not always easy to stay on one's wakeful level and refrain from putting one project against another. For instance, if you have to choose among three projects, of which one is more closely affiliated to you than the other two, will you let honesty and fairness prevail in your ultimate choice, or will you fall prey to favoritism? This is a hard part of being an Awakened Leader, especially when loved ones are involved.

Time Constraints

As a final note: It may also be hard to be an Awakened Leader when there's much to be done in little time, and you have to make prioritizing choices in projects to handle and projects to turn down. It may get tempting to choose the easiest way out or make an ethical slip in those moments. Yet, if you elevate your mental self to a higher consciousness, keep your calm, and let honesty and fairness prevail, then the difficult may become easy and turn out for the good of all, not just for one person.

In Review

In this chapter we reviewed a number of behavioral traits that that can complicate the practice of Awakened Leadership. The difficult elements reviewed in this chapter were:

- Pressure and Politics
- Uncooperativeness and Standards
- Ego Management
- Remaining Authentic
- Inner-Connection
- Incompatibility
- Consistency
- Accountability
- Material Rewards
- Yielding
- Preferences
- Time Constraints

As promised in the Chapter 7 review section, Figure 8.1 provides an overview of the easy and hard aspects in the performance of Awakened Leadership.

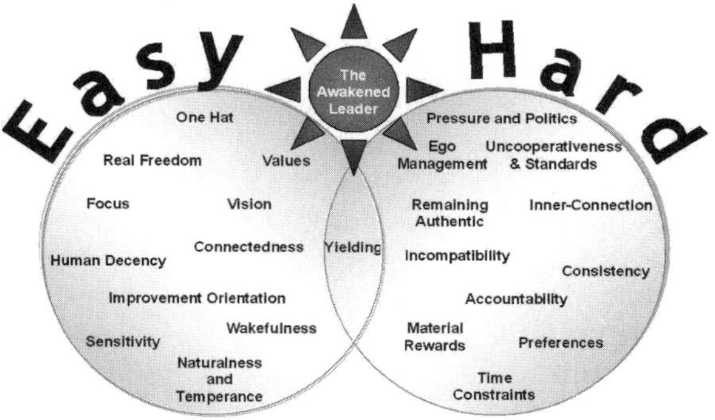

Figure 8.1: **Easy and Hard Aspects of Awakened Leadership Performance**

These are some points I want to remember from this chapter:

My personal opinions after reading this chapter:

Chapter 9:
Essential Issues for an Awakened Leader

All that we are is the result of
what we have thought.
The mind is everything.
What we think we become.
Buddha

What's Ahead

This chapter sums up essential focal points in the pursuit of Awakened Leadership. Stripped of all details, this chapter provides you with clear guidelines for unifying your life and your leadership, so that they become one. The chapter will place conscientious questions and present a self-reflection exercise to help you maintain wakefulness in every part of your life.

It should be clear by now that Awakened Leaders live by their principles in every environment: at work, at home, and in other settings. Yet, they do so in a way that's not experienced as "my way or the highway," because the awakened way is *sensitive*, *cooperative*, and *communicative.* In this chapter we'll briefly review some essential imperatives for your practice of Awakened Leadership.

- Immerse yourself in a deep connection with your spiritual core, and consequentially, into the unity of leading and being. In other words, the way you *lead* should be the way you *are*: authentic, spontaneous, and honest. Remember Gandhi: "I do what I say, I say what I think, and I think what I feel."

- Focus on your relationships with yourself, your family, your colleagues, the communities in which you work and live, and with the universe, knowing that everything else comes as a result of these relationships. If the relationships are good, positive results will follow. If they're disturbed, the results may be less rewarding.

- Pursue health in all important areas of your life:

- ✓ Personal: Allot regular time for practices that will cleanse your soul, enrich your spirit, and revitalize your body. Remain alert to the importance of being healthy in mind, spirit, and body, and know that this health will result in better decision-making, greater alertness, and greater capacity toward understanding.

- ✓ Organizational: Focus on the well-being of the organization; realize that lives are at stake in its direction. Ensure a pleasant, rewarding environment for each stakeholder, knowing that this will result in greater performance and, hence, organizational growth and excellence.

- ✓ Relational: Strive to establish good relationships with each individual you encounter and in every environment you reside. Keep your family life decent, your work relationships positive, and your other relationships mutually gratifying.

- ✓ Environmental: Focus particularly on environmental health, knowing what is at stake if the environment is disrupted. Remember, Awakened Leaders won't become involved in a business that structurally pollutes or impoverishes the environment.

- Focus on sustainable results, fairness, and growth for yourself and others. Make one of your main concerns to be loving and caring toward the universe.

- Focus on your value system: your sense of ethics and morality. Analyze these factors carefully in order to evaluate whether they should remain intact, or whether you need to rethink them.

- Focus on your impact on the lives of others, and ensure that it's a good and well-understood one. Contribute and help in every way you can. Don't live your life for yourself alone. Your life is loved and valued by others for its role in the co-creation of betterment. Live, therefore, with the questions: How can I add toward betterment? How can I fully participate in positive creation? Giving, whether financially, intellectually, or spiritually, should be an important focus in your life.

- Focus on non-material rewards, on the inspiration you receive from doing well by doing good, and from guiding others to higher planes. Focus, thus, on upholding your values, and don't get distracted by toxic interference.

- Focus on your goal, on where you're going. Reexamine your conscience constantly and question if you're actually sticking to the course you've set. This is the focus of *reflection* and *expansion*; reflection in the sense of, "Am I still on track?" and expansion in the sense of, "How can I expand my capacity? How can I truly understand another human being? How can I utilize my humanistic perspectives to meet the bottom line?" *Make the focus on reflection and expansion part of your routine!*
  This chapter will end with an exercise you should execute at least twice a year: "*The Self-Reflection Exercise: Finding Meaning*." It can be helpful in every environment you move in. The self-reflection exercise could be crucial in helping you determine whether you still feel in sync with where you are, or whether you should start thinking about some changes.

- Focus on achievement and satisfaction. Engage deeply in figuring out what the source should be for your satisfaction. Think of what you consider satisfying as a business goal, and formulate how you should meet that goal. Is it about size? Is it about being on the New York stock exchange? Is it about product sales or market share? Is it about recognition? What *is* your condition of satisfaction? As an Awakened Leader you need to define that.

In Review

The most effective review for this chapter is to present you with an exercise that you can use to stay focused on Awakened Leadership.

The Self-Reflection Exercise: Finding Meaning

This exercise is an important step on your way to wakefulness. It's not a one-timer, but a deep contemplation, which you should engage in at least twice a year. It's applicable to various areas of your life. Before you begin the exercise, you should concentrate on one area or environment that you'd like to examine.

Step 1—Ask yourself: What is my purpose here?

Step 2—Am I content with this purpose?

- If yes, proceed to step 3.
- If no, start working on a change of direction immediately, be it through obtaining additional education, networking, applying for new jobs—anything to get yourself out of the current slump.

Step 3—Is the purpose that I ascribe to my being here the same as the purpose others see for me (particularly employers, supervisors, and other key individuals)?

- If yes, proceed to step 4.
- If no, ask the conscious questions: Do I care about this disconnect between perspectives? Is the purpose I see for myself still rewarding to me in spite of the incongruence? Remember, there can be dissimilarity in perceived purposes while everyone is still okay with it. In that case you can proceed to step 4. However, if you sense that this incongruence can lead to future troubles, start looking for alternatives.

Step 4—Would I still want to do this if I got less out of it? Am I proud enough of what I do, to the point that I would also feel great if it were to be printed in tomorrow's newspaper?

- If yes, proceed to step 5.
- If no, you might still decide to stay in this situation for a while, but you should start working on your options, because you're clearly not all that content with where you are. Also, keep in mind that even if you're entirely satis-

fied now, circumstances may change in the future.

Step 5—How can I improve the gratification of my purpose

- ***for myself?***
- ***for my colleagues?***
- ***for my employer?***
- ***for the customers I serve?***
- ***for the planet?***

As a consequence to this probing analysis you should wonder: Is there a feasible way to serve all constituents, even if not through one single act?

- If yes: that's great and you can proceed immediately to step 6.
- If no, ask yourself if you're still satisfied with the improvements you can bring about. If satisfied, proceed to the next step; if not entirely satisfied, you should wonder what matters more to you: staying with a relative dissatisfaction, or moving on. You may not be able to keep all the people happy all the time, even if that's your intention.

Step 6—As things seem now, would I still want to do this five or ten years from now?

- If yes, then you've found your meaning, and you're still on the right track.

- If no, continue looking for alternatives: educate yourself, read, network, surf the Internet; keep your eyes and ears wide open to explore potential future purposes.

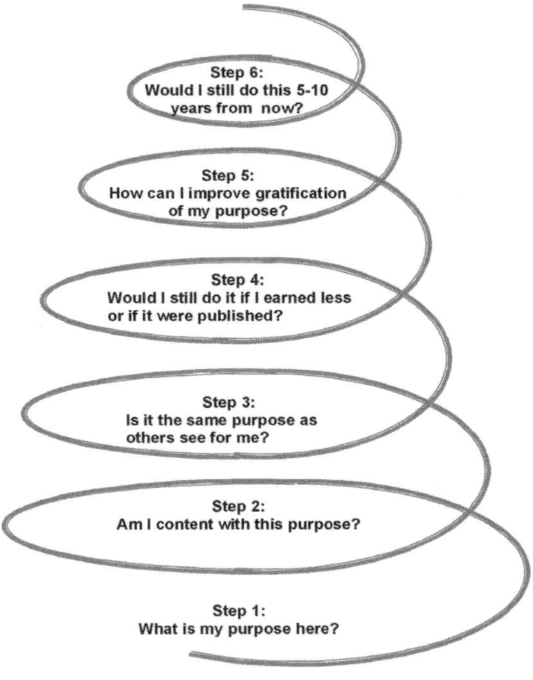

Figure 9.1: **Finding Meaning: The Cycle of Self-Improvement**

These are some points I want to remember from this chapter:
My personal opinions after reading this chapter:

Chapter 10:
Awakened Leadership in Action: A Comparison of 26 Exceptional Business Leaders

Whatever you are, be a good one.
Abraham Lincoln

Among the hundred-plus leaders I interviewed formally and informally for this book, there were 26 business leaders whom I identified as full-fledged Awakened Leaders, and to whom I returned later in order to ask them some specific questions regarding their leadership styles. These individuals, it turned out, were all greatly respected by those who work in their organizations, as well as by most individuals and organizational entities that had any dealings with them through the years.

Some interesting findings surfaced from the interviews with these 26 executives. In this final chapter I present those findings. Keep in mind that, up to this point, the entire book has tried to describe what Awakened Leaders are like. To wit: Awakened Leadership is a meta-leadership style in which you maintain your authenticity and nurture your emotional intelligence, so that you can readily apply every leadership style at your disposal to the right situation, in consideration of all stakeholders.

Following are some interesting similarities among the 26 Awakened Leaders I interviewed.

Qualities

1. They all believe that you can do good (to stakeholders) while doing well (in leading the organization).

2. They exert their decisions and their executive behavior in a dimension that reviews more than the bottom line, but considers enhancing the quality of life as a whole. They believe with this consideration that profits will follow automatically.

3. They're more focused on developing relationships and facilitating people than merely producing a quantifiable product or service: They consider themselves servant leaders when it comes to the people aspect.

4. They understand that motivating employees does not only make these employees feel better about themselves, but also elevates their willpower toward enhanced productivity.

5. They understand the importance of family and try to allow their employees every opportunity to sustain a balance between the workplace and their personal lives.

6. They believe in the power of integrity as a source of community enhancement in their workplace.

7. They're passionate about their work. They love what they do. Therefore, they put their heart into it and exude this contagious attitude toward their co-workers. They're convinced that their passion creates a bond with workers at all levels of their organizations.

8. They maintain high expectations from themselves as well as their co-workers. They work hard yet keep priorities in order. This entails that they can be firm, and even tough at times, but they're also flexible and try to underscore the positives while correcting the negatives.

9. They stay away from toxic situations. They do what it takes to keep their work environment as healthy as possible, so that employees can feel spiritually motivated to attend work, and psychosomatic symptoms as a result of work-related stress remain minimal.

10. They believe in learning. They therefore keep themselves abreast of developments within their organization, within their industry, and within global trends,

and they ensure a pro-learning mentality among their workforces as well.

11. They treat others with respect and dignity, and find that they get treated the same in return.

12. They understand their responsibility as business leaders to take on major issues pertaining to the environment, hunger, and security in a business-like way.

13. Due to the above-listed qualities, they've been able to hold their positions successfully and earn great respect from all stakeholders throughout their careers.

Achievements

The interesting finding about these leaders' perspective on their greatest achievements is that none of them mentioned financial growth as a major milestone. The focus of these individuals was, without exception, on achievements they earned through their relationships with co-workers, mentees, family members, and other persons within and outside of the work environment. They were all proud of the recognition they earned through the years, expressed in the form of awards received on various continents, but they still seemed to find their greatest gratification in seeing those, whose lives they had touched, fulfill their mission and become successful in their own right

Success

Another remarkable finding from the interviews with these 26 executives is that none of them defined success in terms of material affluence. Rather, they emphasized the achievement of goals, set in personal and work-related issues, as their view of success. They clarified that success to them is the satisfaction of being fulfilled in terms of their own values, of witnessing developments that reward and reinforce their values, ethics, morals, beliefs, and convictions. In other words, their main perception of success was the practical reinforcement of what they believed in, in those environments they cared for.

Happiness

These leaders all referred to relationships with family, friends, mentees, co-workers, and nature as their sources of happiness. As in all earlier mentioned examples, none of them considered material abundance a source of happiness. Rather, they equated happiness with inner contentment.

Remembrance

When asked what they wanted to be remembered for, these leaders also provided remarkably similar answers in separate interviews and diverging environments. None of them wanted to be remembered for having built an estate or having earned a fortune, but rather for having been able to contribute positively to the lives of others, whether family, co-workers, or other stakeholders in their lives. They also wanted to be remembered for establishing greater understanding among peoples of various continents, due to their mediation as leaders of organizations that operated among various cultures.

Advice to Other Leaders

The advice these leaders had for other executives follows:

1) To see their responsibility in a much broader way. These leaders felt that there are still too many business executives who have a narrow vision and fail to consider the full responsibility that their company has toward the societies it operates in. They reemphasized that it was eminent for contemporary leaders to consider their liability far beyond the bottom line. They called for more atten-

tion of business leaders toward pressing global matters such as the environment, hunger, and security, as governments have demonstrated an inability to do so in a concerted way.

2) To pay more than lip service to their relationships with employees. It was these leaders' observation that too often leaders' walk does not measure up to their talk. Too many beautiful mission statements remain unexecuted. The leaders interviewed here emphasized in that regard, "If you take good care of your people, they'll take good care of you and your mission."

3) To be more in touch with all levels of their company, and therewith encourage a team spirit and an elevated sense of meaning, resulting in greater satisfaction and translated in increased productivity.

4) To have a corporate culture that addresses humanity as a whole (the stakeholders) rather than just the stockholders.

5) To earn their leadership by executing the qualities listed above, in order to transform leadership from a mere duty to the most rewarding experience.

Based on these interviews, I conclude that these leaders share three primary values:

1. They all take pride in what they do: they love their job and infect their environment with this attitude.
2. They're all very relationship-oriented, without losing sight of the production process or the returns on investment. Rather, by establishing a great connection with their co-workers, they manage to create a work environment of satisfied people and, consequently, optimal output.
3. They understand the value of earning money, but don't prioritize it over everything. Rather, they realize that earnings will be a logical consequence of the two values listed just above: loving their job and loving their people.

In the descriptions of their values, these leaders provided the perfect illustration of what Awakened Leadership is about.

These are some points I want to remember from this chapter:
My personal opinions after reading this chapter:

Epilogue

As a final impulse, I asked twelve individuals whom I identified as having Awakened Leaders' traits what would make them quit their jobs. Here are their answers, clustered in three comprehensive statements:

- If I had a very personal inner feeling that I was part of an organization that did not share my values and what I am, if the culture of that organization was inconsistent with my innermost spirituality, or if I tried to do something and the organization did not take on it, especially when it's about change for the better, or if I would find that I was not equipped to bring about the change that's necessary to guide the organization further, then I would quit my job.

- If I were forced to do something against my philosophy of life, against my ethical principles, or against my foundations for human dignity, I would quit my job. I was once working at a production company, and I was in charge of the budget. I realized that the producer was trying to manipulate the budget, and he thought he could sweet-talk me over it, and I could not bring myself to play along. So I left, for I wouldn't want to be part of something I couldn't agree with. Doing something that goes against my ethical values would make me quit my job.

- Anything that hurts people, including myself, would make me quit my job. Not just the responsibility of hiring and firing, because that's part of the job, but if something would be hurtful, I'd have a problem with it. A commander-in-chief has to be active and decisive, and people get hurt in that process. There's nothing to do about that. But if we live in harmony with our principles, we would not be hurting people deliberately. I would look for a more nurturing environment. As long as I could see fulfillment and satisfaction and progress, and fun and pleasure, I would not leave.

The above points that would make the interviewed Awakened Leaders quit their jobs can be summarized in three categories:

1) *Incompatibility* between your ways and the company's goals, culture, or processes;
2) *Ethical conflicts;*
3) *Hurtful practices*.

To sum up, Figure 10.1 illustrates the points made in Chapter 9, essential issues for an Awakened Leader, and these end remarks based on issues that would make an Awakened Leader quit his or her job.

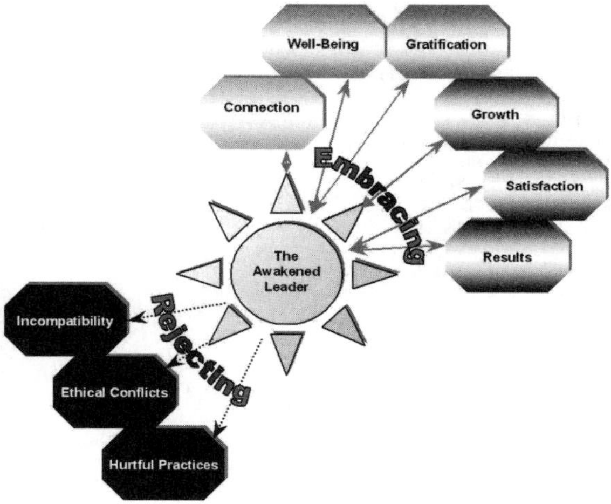

Figure 10.1: **What's in It – Or Not – for the Awakened Leader**

Index

About the Author

Joan Marques has authored/co-authored five books. *Empower the Leader in You* and *The Global Village* were published in 2004. *The Awakened Leader, Spirituality in the Workplace,* and *Seasoned Adages for Modern Days' Leaders* were published in 2007.

She lectures Business and Management at Woodbury University, and is co-initiator and editor-in-chief of three scholarly/practical journals: *The Business Renaissance Quarterly (BRQ), The Journal of Global Business Issues (JGBI),* and *Global Watch.* She holds leadership positions in the Business Renaissance Institute and MDG Global Watch.

Prior to her American experience, Joan enjoyed more than 20 successful years in media production in Suriname, South America. She founded and managed an advertising and public relations company, and a foundation for women's advancement. In her position as advocate for women's issues and a prominent master of ceremonies, she guided and executed NGO- and government-related presentations in Suriname, Guyana, and the Netherlands Antilles.

In 1998, Joan migrated to Burbank, California, and embarked upon a journey of continuing education and inspiration. She holds a B.Sc. in Business Economics, an MBA, and a Doctorate in Organizational Leadership, as well as various certificates of leadership, women's advocacy, media writing, presenting, and leading.

Joan writes articles on a wide range of topics. Most of these writings can be found on the Internet.

She is also a poet, and plans to bring out her first book of poetry soon.

Joan Marques is the proud mother of Coert Jr., Evita, and Mercedes Nelson, and grandmother of Jo-Anne.

DATE DUE

Jan 5/	10		